Boundaries of Intelligence

Senses and Spirituality in Management

Nilton Bonder

Order this book online at www.trafford.com
or email orders@trafford.com

Most Trafford titles are also available at major online book retailers.

Printed in Victoria, BC, Canada.

ISBN: 978-1-4269-2617-4 (Soft)
ISBN: 978-1-4269-2618-1 (Hard)

Library of C0ngress Control Number: 2010901047

*Our mission is to efficiently provide the world's finest, most comprehensive
book publishing service, enabling every author to experience success.
To find out how to publish your book, your way, and have it available
worldwide, visit us online at www.trafford.com*

Trafford rev. 02/12/2010

www.trafford.com

North America & international
toll-free: 1 888 232 4444 (USA & Canada)
phone: 250 383 6864 ♦ fax: 812 355 4082

'It is harder to find a disciple than a rabbi. Because making someone believe is easier than believing. Giving is easier than receiving. In short, being an apprentice is more human than being a master.'

Rabbi Yitschak Yaakov,
The Seer of Lublin

To
André, Samantha, Felipe, Carolina ,Julia and Manuela Schwartz

Contents

Introduction

In recent years, I have given lectures at large corporations around Brazil and in several other countries. I feel a bit awkward whenever I receive these invitations, however, since they come in very abstract and vague proposals. The hosts don't really know how to specify or define what they want. This isn't exactly common in the business world, which in our culture is on the cutting edge of objectivity and pragmatism. What do they want from a rabbi? One's first reaction is: They certainly don't want the kingdom of heaven! But the more I think about what they really want, the more I tend to believe it is precisely the kingdom of heaven that interests them.

Our world has lived in the shadow of ignorance for many centuries. The Age of Darkness is not a term that applies solely to more insidious times like the Middle Age but can be extended to the whole history of our civilization. Yet this perverse benightedness has its holy manifestation as well. The shadow of shadow is light. We realize this if we stay in the dark very long, for our eyes begin to see hidden lights. This is, after all, what we experience at the end of every afternoon, when darkness reveals the stars and lights that the brightness of day prevented us from seeing (*Psalm 36:09*).

We are starting to see better in the dark. We know the human being better than ever before, because we have learned from our cumulative suffering—for 'the reward of suffering is experience' (*Aeschylus*). Through its accumulated experiences, humanity has revealed its weaknesses and greatnesses, its limitations and inspirations, its fears and dreams. We stand more naked than ever before.

Companies searching for their 'earthly kingdom' have discovered that the intelligence of the 'kingdom of heaven' can be useful in terms of efficiency, and in a highly competitive world nobody can afford to ignore a form of intelligence. In our days, we have begun to recognize a universe that until just recently was considered to lie outside the realm of categories of intelligence.

The present book endeavors to exemplify this type of intelligence along with some of the rules governing its 'logic'. Don't shy away from criticizing it, just as it is legitimate to question any form of intelligence. However, be intelligent enough to understand that the light of this intelligence is that which comes from darkness. Differently from regular light which produces shadow, the clarity of spiritual intelligence can only be taken advantage of in dense gloom. That is why its equations have been couched in the form of parables and stories. This manner of organizing notions and theories stirs the subconscious to produce the shadow needed for the light of this intelligence to make itself visible.

Intelligence and our reading of reality

Who is intelligent? The sages respond by saying: 'Whoever learns from every human being.' Wisdom is not knowledge but the ability to learn.

There is no way of truly responding to a question without delving deeper into the original question.

Nobel prize-winning chemist Karl Ziegler, when asked why he had become so outstanding in his field, responded saying that his mother was to thank for his accomplishments. He told how she would pick him up after school and instead of posing the question all parents invariably put to their children —'What did you <u>learn</u> at school today?' —, she would inquire — 'What did you <u>ask</u> in school today?'. What makes a difference is this restlessness and interest in doubt, because such an attitude prepares a person to learn from every human being and from every opportunity in life. This is the aptitude the Talmud classifies as 'intelligence.'

The only way to reach certainty is through doubt. And even so, this certainty must forever stay open to doubt. In other words, it must remain in the category of doubt. Spirituality is no exception to this rule of intelligence. Contrary to what many think, faith is not composed of certainties but of doubts we work through in a sensitive and sophisticated fashion. Faith is a reading of reality using the most subtle and subjective tools of human intellect.

The intellect displays four types of aptitudes:

- Information: Literal Sphere / Storage in memory
- Understanding: Analytical Sphere / Analysis of information
- Intuition or Interstanding :
  Symbolic Sphere / Analysis of understandings
- Reverence: Sphere of Beliefs / Analysis of intuitions

Information and understanding are attributes of the brain's left hemisphere, while intuition and reverence are attributes of the right. What differentiates them, however, is the degree of doubt assigned to certainty. The greater the degree of doubt within a given certainty, the closer it will come to reality. It is true that a certainty's degree of operability and practical usefulness decreases as the degree of doubt increases. Nevertheless, as we will see next, our world has a growing need for people trained in profound degrees of doubt, more so than for people skilled at handling certainties.

The Talmud in the tractate of *Pirkei Avot* exemplifies this notion in the following terms: *"I have learned much from my teachers, even more from my peers, but above all from my students"*. Learning is greater when doubts and uncertainties are present. A teacher represents the authority of knowledge, which decreases at the level of a peer, and then decreases further at the level of a student. The teacher is understanding; the peer, intuition; and the student, reverence.

It is essential for us to define these terms, particularly because the one that causes greatest perplexity is precisely the one that interests us most: reverence. Not reverence in the sense of obedience or veneration but in the sense of an ability to recognize and prioritize certain principles of life.

Students sometimes used to be given a test that had only two questions on it, one where pupils would consequently receive a grade of either 100, 50, or zero. The contrast between a score of 100 and one of zero was so striking that it would be hard to understand how two individuals with similar IQ's could receive such opposite grades.

In point of fact, these tests were a good definition of the difference between information and understanding. Some students in a classroom only pay attention so they will later be able to solve a problem. These are the ones busy taking notes. But there are other pupils, less concerned with seizing hold of information and certainty and more interested in doubts. The first kind of student will know how to solve test problems that are just like those the teacher has gone over in class. The second kind will have no trouble solving problems that have undergone some modification, because he understands the principles behind the classroom solutions.

In order to illustrate the passage from the sphere of understanding to that of intuition, let's look at another kind of result obtained in life: success. How many times have you run across someone driving a flashy car who used to be a poor student? Rich and successful, the latter individual stands out from the good student who leads a mediocre life, devoid of great achievements or recognition. How can this be possible? The answer is that the good student became trapped in the world of understanding, while the other made felicitous incursions into the world of intuition.

We are crossing the boundary dividing the two halves of the brain. On this other side, being and experience contribute as much to efficiency as do theory and models on the left side. Understanding is limited to analysis, and no matter how many indexes or trends understanding may detect, it grows imprecise in the realm of risk and uncertainty. Because understanding is the expected result, all phenomena and events that cannot be understood are discarded as useless and inefficacious.

Why did the poor student turn out so successful? Because he learned to stay more open to doubts than did the student devoted to understanding. For an assortment of reasons, the good student—the one who understood—cast aside doubts and went after certainties. *But it is the act of delving deeper into doubt that makes success possible.* Even when there are no certainties to be understood, intuition perceives certain trends and certain types of logic that can be proven only through practical application and risk-taking.

What distinguishes understanding from intuition is that the first answers a question with another question in order to arrive at a certainty. The second, however, doesn't expect any certainty but instead answers a question with another question in order to arrive at a doubt. This doubt lies closer to reality than the certainties of someone who understands, and therefore it is more efficacious and will lead to victories and success.

Moving at last to the sphere of reverence, let us look at another kind of result obtained in life: peace and happiness. How are we to understand it when a successful man or woman, who enjoys the best life has to offer, is unhappy or even miserable? Perhaps it is because a person may become skeptical or even cynical when he or she relinquishes certainty in order to master and manipulate doubt. This is the difference between someone intuitive and someone who displays reverence. The latter not only endeavors to remain in the cloudy world of doubt but in the midst of it asks whether certainties might not exist. It is this doubt about doubt that produces 'reverences.' And their efficiency can be measured in terms of quality of life.

We can synthesize these notions as follows:

- Information = certainties
- Understanding = doubts assigned to certainties
- Intuition = certainties assigned to doubts
- Reverence = doubts assigned to doubts

Someone who acts in reverence accepts doubts about doubts themselves. This means the world of uncertainties will have doubts about itself. Is there some kind of continuation after death? Is there an order that flows through all Creation? Is there a Creator? To answer these questions, you must immerse yourself in doubt, in order to doubt doubts themselves. It is impossible to reach such 'certainties' by the path of certainties. Does God exist? From the angle of certainty, or of science, the most plausible answer is 'no.' Is death the end? According to this same criterion, we'd have to say 'yes.' But who respects these rational answers? Our sensibilities are more interested in hearing from those who search among doubts than from those who fixate on certainties.

In other words, there is a world of brightness and another of shadow. Trying to illuminate the world of shadow robs it of its efficiency. In shadow, our eyes begin to see in a way that brightness does not allow us. When darkness falls, whoever lives in the clarity of light is blinded. Those who are used to shadow have no trouble making out shapes in the dark. The problem with what is clear and visible is that *our eyes see only what our minds are ready to understand.* Only certainty is visible. Learning to see beyond it means acquiring distinct new skills.

Intuition and reverence are outlines. It is the nature of reverence to be nothing but an outline. Whenever we attempt to fill it in, it vanishes. The certainty that comes from doubting doubt is grounded on the idea that whatever is not certain—shadow—is always the product of a light source. Shadow is not light itself but it indicates the place from which light emanates. Turning your eyes towards this light of lights means engaging yourself spiritually.

Spirituality and Employability

When the brain is needed, muscles won't do.
When the heart is needed, the brain won't do.
When the soul is needed, the heart won't do.

A word that has been gaining importance is 'employability.' The nineteenth and twentieth centuries were times of jobs and salaries. But the future seems intent on relegating this form of sustenance to the memory and museums of human civilization. We are returning to a model closer to nature, where competitiveness gives no one an *a priori* guarantee about receiving a certain wage at the end of every month. This kind of promise leads to the subjugation and exploitation of people; it causes countries and their social security systems to go bankrupt; and, above all, it engenders inefficacious processes of production and creation.

Human progress has in fact moved towards correcting this distortion left from the early industrial period. We have created ways of doing away with wage earners, and now the world faces the ensuing crisis at the dawn of the twenty-first century.

Industrialization is based on the idea that consumption will rise steadily—for a finite planet, a highly questionable notion both in practical as well as mathematical terms. An economy that produces ever greater quantities needs to create masses of consumers. The system's wage earners are the very ones who leverage this consumption, like a kind of perpetual motion machine driven more by human naïveté and greed than by any profound perception of reality. The static concept of 'having a job' is gradually being replaced by more dynamic models, more coherent with life itself, where we make ourselves either 'employable' or not.

And what kind of person is employable in this new model? Certainly the least employable is someone who possesses only information. The technician—almost an extension of a manual laborer—is being replaced by machines. Computers and information networks are technicians *par excellence*, available 24 hours a day, always. They are available in the memory banks of our civilization. Technicians are replaceable, and they are being replaced.

But it's not just them. Those who played the role of 'understanding' processes—managers—are also becoming cog pieces from the past. Since understanding belongs to the sphere of certainty, machines will also take over the activity of understanding and managing. If machines can play chess, why shouldn't they be able to manage? Under the traditional model, managers will soon be unemployed.

Part of the reason companies invite me to give lectures is that the labor market is looking for 'intuitive' people and 'reverential' people. Human employability will be defined in areas where we are skilled and offer a competitive advantage over machines: the areas of doubt and uncertainty. Only something that experiences can display intuitive intelligence and reverence. Machines can only compete in these spheres if we make them come alive, turning them into human or super-human beings. For this to happen, machines need to experience (among other things) finitude and reproduction, two of life's essential issues.

The world of the future will therefore be seeking out 'intuitives' and 'reverentials.' Perhaps it is easier to understand the first. He acts as a member of the board or as a partner in more modern companies. This employee runs calculated risks and participates in them. He uses his experience to build bridges between certainties slashed through by doubts. This process entails creation, involvement, integration, art, vision, confidence, and risk. Whoever knows how to accomplish it will have no trouble finding a place on the twenty-first century's labor market.

The second person—the reverential—epitomizes the labor power of the future. The reverential worker not only does the job of the intuitive worker; he is also a *strategist of intuition.* The realization that our planet is finite and that all of life on it is interconnected set in motion last century's ecological consciousness-raising process. But we have only attained a tiny fraction of the consciousness level that will be reached in the future. Ecology contributed greatly to establishing spiritual concepts for the market and for politicians. This is because talk of finitude and the perception of the interconnectedness of life reflect concepts of spirituality, as we will see later. Ecology is nothing more than a form of reverence. In it, we recognize one of life's deep structures, and we offer it our desire to adapt so we do not run the risk of being excluded from it.

In the future, the 'employee' with an ecological consciousness will not be a subversive who jeopardizes the interests of his company or economy, as is still the case today. Rather, he will be indispensable because all products' efficiency will also be measured by how well they are suited to strategies that favor and enhance life. In other words, a consumer who buys a product that doesn't harm the ozone layer, and is today seen as a romantic, tomorrow will simply be complying with a law enacted by ecologically responsible, conscious authorities. This is not fiction but the realization of an absolute law of economics—the law of supply and demand. When the demand for life assumes a certain form, whoever can provide it will find they have a vast market.

All this may seem well beyond our reality and, in certain areas more than others, it is. But notice how those who have managed to develop 'reverences' are benefiting from higher employability ratings. The search for ethical individuals, or those concerned with ethics, is now rising and can be expected to accelerate even more sharply. The 'designers' of reverences for governments, corporations, or any active human organization will be the builders of the future. In fact, every worker will need to establish his or her own reverences in order to survive.

No work and no contribution to society will be possible without at least the rudiments of spirituality.

What Is Spirituality?

Spirituality has always been a product of human restlessness and doubt. It asks three main questions that other forms of intelligence avoid or deal with only superficially or pragmatically: 'Where do we come from?', 'What is our purpose?', and 'Where do we go?'

Such questions may seem irrelevant if we think solely in terms of the quest for efficiency through information, understanding, and intuition. These questions mean nothing when it comes to getting something right, solving something, or being successful at something. Yet they are fundamental to attaining peace and happiness.

Peace and happiness are the feelings that come when you have no balances outstanding in the realm of duties and rights. If you don't give properly of yourself or don't receive from others in the appropriate measure, you will not find peace or happiness. *Reverencing means being aware of certain principles of life and knowing how to value and place priority on them*—principles that constitutes the central concerns of spirituality. What are these principles?

The mystic Lawrence Kushner categorizes spirituality's main tenets into six essential reverences:

1. Reality is made up of various layers.
2. The world is but a passage.
3. Everything is interconnected.
4. You are in all the Universe and all the Universe is in you.
5. Everything is Nothing.
6. We are all part of the Universe's process of transformation.

Spirituality is the intelligence based on uncertainty, which results in the six tenets above. Notice these tenets most probably make sense to us, although we can't prove any one of them. The task of someone who acts in reverence is to design individual and collective policies and plans of action employing these six tenets as reference points.

Control × Presence

Another way of defining intelligence is by ascertaining someone's ability to make connections or establish relations. In terms of logic, this means 'bananas plus bananas and apples plus apples.' A relationship, however, in its broadest sense, involves an ongoing process of contact and encounter between one element and another. It is a relationship that allows a small gear to be part of an entire mechanism. The gear's existence does not suffice to render it real and efficacious. These qualities can only derive from the relationship it establishes with the parts around it.

It is relationship that makes possible the state of 'presence'—that is, being in a certain place at a certain time. And presence is the only way we can accomplish the very purpose of our existence.

Everyone will agree that the best time to try to close a business deal is not when you're sleepy. When doing business, you want to be alert, present, and attuned to any situation that might arise. So it is with presence in its broadest sense. Whoever is not only intellectually present but emotionally and spiritually present as well will be better equipped to act on reality.

But how can we intensify presence? Presence is directly related to the loss of control: the greater your control, the lesser your presence. Presence is your willingness to be in relationship to, and this happens only during the moment itself. The more we prepare ourselves and the less spontaneous we are because we have worked out strategies and expectations, the lesser our ability to relate to a given moment. We will be predisposed and, under these circumstances, less alert to the unexpected opportunities and situations that may occur.

Even so, it is important to stress that this process of presence of course does not exclude rationality nor even certain aspects of control. Control may be an instrument but not the vehicle of presence. The vehicle, or means, by which we place ourselves in relationship with whatever is around us, is lack of control.

The gauge that serves to measure presence is surprise. Every efficacious process should produce surprising aspects and situations. When surprise is absent, when we try to control reality by anticipating presence, we experience a loss of 'intelligence' and, consequently, of quality of life.

> *In Jewish tradition, there are two words used to signify the idea of happiness: 'sasson' and 'simcha'. The second term denotes the satisfaction we feel when all is in order and under control. A birthday party is a simcha—a happy event that has been planned and scheduled to take place on a certain day and at a certain time. 'Sasson', on the other hand, refers to the surprised happiness brought by some unexpected pleasure. To experience this kind of happiness we must not exaggerate our measure of control.*

Portuguese has a word that shares the same root as the English word 'joy': *jóia*. Literally, it means 'jewel' or 'gem'. But in 1980s slang, it recouped its original root sense and gained the connotation of spontaneous, surprised jubilation. Etymologically, the meaning was profound, expressing openness to surprise. It was like a declaration: 'I'm so fine for I'm ready to be present here and enjoy whatever this moment gives me.' The utilization of presence is always the instrument that leads us to happiness, which in itself is the end goal of any 'intelligent' process.

We can now understand how intelligence and presence is the same thing, and that presence is a gauge of relationship to the external world. The deeper this relationship is, the greater the intelligence. What that means is that a person's capacity for 'encounters' is a gauge of intelligence. Therein lies the secret of the poor student who proves a success. He compensates for his limited capacity to draw rational relations by utilizing his capacity to maintain genuine physical, emotional, and spiritual relationships. Whoever achieves happiness and peace is certainly more skilled in the art of intelligence or—as we can now put it—in the art of being present.

Encounters and Intelligence

Distinguishing between pictures, windows, doors, and portals

'It is told that two important Hasidic rabbis were invited to co-officiate at a wedding—Rabbi Levi Yitzchak of Berditchev and the Alter Rebbe, Rabbi Shneur Zalman. Each possessed distinct personality traits. Rabbi Levi was known as an extremely spontaneous person, whose soul was pure fire. For him the world did not exist, only the reality of God. The Alter Rebbe, on the other hand, of course considered God very important, but for him the world and its reality existed as well. When he prayed, Rabbi Levi moved about the synagogue so much that at one moment he was here and an instant later, somewhere else. But the Alter Rebbe would remain in one same spot. On the day of the wedding, when they were both heading to the room where the ceremony would take place, the two rabbis found themselves before a very narrow door, through which both could not pass side by side. Out of customary politeness, one said to the other, 'Please, after you.' The other refused: 'No, no, after you.' They remained like that for a few moments, until Rabbi Levi finally said: 'We shall go through the

---

1   Hasidism: A Jewish movement of spiritual renewal founded by Israel ben Eliezer (1698-1760), the Baal Shem Tov, in the early half of the eighteenth century, in Central Europe. This movement revived mystical practices including the Kabbalah, as well as songs, dances, and, above all, legends and fables that portray these communities' ethics and world view.

> *wall!' To which the Alter Rebbe replied: 'No—all we need to do is widen the door.'*
>
> *(as told by Rabbi Schlomo Carlebach Z'L)*

What is special about this story is its very important and precise definition of the concept of portals—for these create the conditions prerequisite to encounters. Making recourse to the image of a house with doors and walls, our story serves to call attention to differences, or better put, to individuality. The starting point for all relationships and therefore all types of intelligence are the boundaries of our being, of our individuality. We are all inside a house, and this home sweet home is our Self.

Our 'home' is made up of spatial separations and demarcations. That is its purpose, to wit, to afford us protection and safety through these limits. But ways of communicating with the outer world are still necessary. If there are none, the house becomes a prison and instead of protecting and fostering life, it becomes destructive.

There are four ways of creating openings and means of communication beyond this delimited space: 1) pictures; 2) windows; 3) doors; and 4) portals. As we will see later on, these forms of communication correspond to different kinds of relationships with the outer world and, as such, to four different levels of intelligence.

The first—the picture—is a false kind of communication. Pictures can depict lovely landscapes of fields and forests but they are static and do not allow us any true interaction. Although they produce a sensation of greater breadth and less imprisonment than a demarcated space, this communication is an illusion. Pictures represent an 'I-it' relationship, where there is no true possibility of communication with the real world. We can imagine and fantasize through a picture but any exchange with the canvas happens from us to us. There is room for richness and art in an exchange with a picture, but this is not a relationship of presence and loss of control since no Other is involved.

These are relationships of total control. They offer a pretense of external reality but no true opening to this reality.

There's a story about two competing companies who decided to extend their rivalry into the athletic area. They organized an 8-plus crew regatta—that is, eight people rowing and one calling the strokes. The winning team beat the other by many lengths. The defeated company decided to hire the top consultants to ascertain why they had lost by so much. After months of thoroughgoing analysis, the specialists concluded: 'You lost because the other side had eight people rowing and one in command, while you had eight in command and only one rowing.' What would the solution be then? The consultants were assigned to devise strategies for correcting the problem. After some further months of studies, they concluded: 'To improve the team's performance, the fellow who is rowing should do it harder and faster.'

Here there is no way intelligence can interact with reality. The desire for control (and consultants are often the prime instrument of this sentiment in the professional arena) precludes any solution that would meddle with structures and concepts; the solution must be found within an environment free of 'encounter' or risk. This means the solution will never entail a process but merely be the expression of a desire.

Windows, on the other hand, are a real opening onto the outer world, although they do not let us enter and exit it. We see the outer world through them, and it sees us as well. But reality stays at a remove from us. Windows can surprise us but we are still protected by separation and control—I see what's going on outside but it's not happening to me. Televisions are windows. And screens, particularly the Internet, are 'windows'. They let us engage in an experience where a certain degree of control is lost, an experience we call 'virtual'. Something virtual may even be perceived as a kind of relationship but it is a very limited sort of presence, because the Other becomes controllable. All you have to do is close the window or not open it and the Other, surprise, and interaction all disappear. The Other has no face and at our whim can be transformed into an 'it'.

Doors put us face to face with the Other. We can close them, or not open them, but once they are open, they not only allow us to exit through them but let the world come in through them. This presence is genuine, and through it we see a less idealized reality. People are better and worse than we imagined. We ourselves are worse and better than we imagined. And it is in these categories—better and worse—that surprise is expressed. We are thus surprised by others and by ourselves. Such encounters through doors produce greater intelligence. At the same time, because a door exposes, it places the 'house' at a real risk. It is not uncommon for people to install locks and all sorts of safety devices, which is a recognition that the 'house' and control become vulnerable to the surprise existing in presence and in encounters.

It is through portals, however, that spiritual intelligence makes itself present. Portals symbolize a radical presence, commonly associated with intense feelings of desegregation and loss of control. Portals are doors that in and of themselves can be a surprise—they can be wider than at first thought or even eliminate the concept of walls and suggest 'going through them.' It is this collapse in our sense of house that underlies the fear of desegregation provoked by portals. But it is not a total collapse, for even widened doors or permeable walls still preserve some structure of 'house', or of individuality.

Every moment of creativity, inspiration, and genius depends upon these widened doors or vanishing walls. In order to experience this, we need walls that can vanish or give way to bigger doors, without losing our sense of house. It is this sense of house—even when thrown open to external reality—that constitutes a 'reverence'.

In this larger encounter with what lies outside ourselves—at the edge of loss of our own identity, owing to so much identification and contact with what lies outside ourselves—that a very special form of intelligence results. It is a journey beyond our mental blocks and illusions, and it brings us in close touch with reality.

Senses and Reverences

Our senses are the most important instruments in our journey and navigation through life. They are our constant points of reference in any action we take, even though we don't understand them well. We believe they constitute rational thought processes whereas they are really basic reference points built out of our own experiences. Our sense of balance, our sense of direction, our sense of propriety and so many other senses are formed from the minute adjustments and corrections made possible by experience as we leave ourselves open to things and take risks.

Most of the time, we don't realize our decisions are based primarily on these senses. Contrary to what many argue, our decisions are not the products of rational decision-making processes. A wide array of so-called decision-making techniques is heralded today, as if we could reach the most important decisions by framing strategies and employing logic. The aim of such rational decision-making processes is to keep risks as low as possible, but when risks are reduced, so too are creativity and intelligence at some level. The resultant decisions can be 'windows' at most or, under the best circumstances, 'doors'. They will never realize the potential of becoming 'portals'. Our ability to widen doors or pass through walls depends definitively upon our use of these senses.

Our navigation through life involves a process of deciding, doing, and only then explaining. Explanation is always the last stage because it serves as our justification. But the explanation does not account for the real reason behind a given decision. The two may at times coincide but the explanation constitutes a third moment in our experience. Our initial decision is based on the sophisticated instruments we call senses.

This means that refining our senses is the best way of reaching the most appropriate decisions, the ones that will take us farthest towards what we want for ourselves and our world. The parameters guiding these senses are what I call 'reverences'. In empty space, the rabbis said, there is no right nor left but only a 180° turn that heads us in the opposite direction. Knowing which the direction is and which the opposite direction is constitutes the spiritual world's binary system (0 or 1). What we hold in reverence and what we don't are the only parameters pertinent to our senses.

Senses and Counter-senses

Going the wrong way

More than constituting expressions of logic, our senses reflect possibilities. A possibility that becomes a reality is soon viewed as something obvious, normal—but it is important for us to remember that up until then it was not. Senses, unlike certainties, find their nourishment in exceptions and counter-senses. When a disciple asks his master how he can develop good sense, he hears the following answer: 'Good sense comes from experience, and experience comes from bad sense.' In other words, good sense comes from bad sense.

This is what a portal is all about. A portal challenges something which has until that moment been deemed an impossibility. People who many times have run into walls acquire the incredible skill of being able go through them. What we often admire in masters and what we view as magic or super-human is their ability to do things we consider impossible. What we fail to see is the profound process of running into walls that eventually allowed them to find a portal.

These efficacious impossibilities are what help us persevere in our quest to find portals. Every experience that defeats us, that tears apart our conceptions and perceptions, is a revealing experience. Such experiences not only gradually equip us to deal with life more openly and efficaciously but also foster belief and reverence. If so many portals exist, if so many ways of going through a wall or widening a doorway exist, who knows what may be possible—things that seem impossible to us today.

This learning takes place by our going the wrong way. Doing the opposite of whatever our good sense tells us, and realizing that this is truly good sense, is the most efficacious way to refine and enhance our senses.

It is said that a Jewish storeowner in the southern United States, in a small town where the Ku Klux Klan had strong roots, became the target of young boys who would throw stones at his shop. Under the influence of racism, these boys saw the small business as a perfect target. At the end of the day, the shopkeeper came out and in a menacing voice asked the boys, 'Who's been throwing rocks at my store all day?' At first fearful they would be taken to task, the boys soon recovered their confidence and began to confess: 'Me…me…and me—why? What are you going to do about it?' The businessman took a bundle of dollar bills out of his pocket and gave one to each child who had confessed. The boys didn't understand anything, and ran off to their homes.

The next day, twice as many children were throwing stones. When it came time to close up shop, the same thing repeated itself. The owner walked out to the boys and asked the same question: 'Who's been throwing rocks at my store all day?' The boys were quick to admit their guilt. The man took some money from his pocket and gave everyone who confessed fifty cents.

The next day there was an amazing number of children throwing stones. And once again, when closing time came, the shopkeeper repeated his question: 'Who's been throwing stones at my store?' The small crowd fought among themselves to confess first: 'Me…me…me!' The man then took some money out of his pocket and began handing out dimes. The boys looked at the coins with contempt and responded alike: 'What? You expect us to spend the whole day throwing stones for a lousy ten cents?!' They left in disgust and never came back.

It's hard to go against our senses, and acting against our perceptions—which often are no more than disguised interests—is just as hard. What the shopkeeper did by paying those who were damaging his property was not a counter-sense, as it might first appear. He realized how the boys' stone throwing was devoid of any real meaning or intention. If he had questioned their actions or gotten into an argument with them, it would have lent legitimacy to their empty desire to throw stones. What the shopkeeper did instead was lend a new 'intent' to the act. The boys came to believe their purpose was payment, and the payment kept decreasing until they were disgusted by its low value.

The storeowner was able to spot a portal because he managed to relate to the situation in a way that was alive. The circumstances did not simply constitute a picture or a window but a real issue, and as such they demanded creative, intuitive interactions and solutions.

Here's another example of how we can achieve our purposes by 'going the wrong way':

> *A truck full of merchandise was being unloaded in front of a store, but the businessman had no invoices to show for the goods. The workers had barely begun taking things off the truck when the police pulled up and two officers got out. The workers ran into the store in alarm, crying: 'The police are here... We've just started unloading and we don't have any invoices. What are we going to do?' The owner showed no worry. 'Go back out there and slowly start to load the truck again,' he said. Although the men had no idea how this would solve the problem, they did as they were told. Meanwhile, the officers approached them and asked: 'What is it you're loading into the truck? Have you got the necessary paperwork?' The workers said they didn't. The police were quick to respond: 'You can start unloading this stuff right now. It's not going any place!'*

Being wise enough to not swim against the tide—an attitude that helps drowning people save their own lives by momentarily letting themselves go with the flow of the sea—is a profound counter-sense. All true senses are like such finely calibrated scopes that they need not fear aiming at themselves or pointing away from the apparent target, for this is merely a way of taking a short-cut.

Life requires such behavior of us all the time. It's hard for us to admit it because our desire for control keeps us from giving in to the tide. But our physical, emotional, intellectual, and spiritual survival depends upon such decisions that seem to head us in the wrong direction. They allow us to assimilate life's contradictions—and especially our misfortunes—as temporary mechanisms of survival. It is by stumbling and by losing control that we achieve greater control. In other words, if we want to attain more peace and 'control', we have to head in the other direction, detaching ourselves not only from our preconceived ideas but also from our very conceptions. Doors are the domain of preconceptions. Portals require us to relinquish even our conceptions.

We are going to journey into different areas of our experience in order to examine some important senses. We will see that all true senses have a north, a 'magnetic' reference point that merges with the real reason why things are the way they are. This north is reverence and spirituality. The focal point of any sense flows into /* ends up within this dimension, and this is the very definition of spirituality, the ultimate reason that motivates us.

Sense of Self

Replacing 'What I am' with 'Who I am'

The Rabbi of Premishlan said:

> *When a horse goes to drink from a pond, he beats his hoof in the water. Do you know why? Because he sees his reflection and imagines that there's another horse also trying to drink. He beats his hoof to try to frighten the 'other' horse off. Every single one of us, like this horse, lives in fear of his own reflection, and we refuse to understand that it is all a reflection of the Creator. The more we beat our hooves, the stronger the other looks to us. Sometimes we even keep from drinking the water out of fear of this other.*

Fear is the greatest obstacle for our sense of self. In the final analysis, what we are always afraid of is losing ourselves. We don't realize that the fear of losing ourselves from ourselves is what creates the very sense of self we are so afraid of losing. And like a vicious circle, if we quit fearing, our sense of self would likewise disappear.

Our sense of self and fear are always linked, like our sense of self and suffering. The greater our sense of self, the greater our fear and terror—and the greater our terror, the greater our suffering. If we were to relinquish our sense of self, the fear would go away; if the fear went away, we would no longer have a sense of self.

So what is the way out of this vicious circle? The secret lies in freeing ourselves from the drama of 'I' and of 'mine.' And it is here that the sense of a Creator can be so important.

> *The story goes that a disciple knocked on the rabbi's door late at night. The master asked: 'Who is it?' The disciple answered: 'It is I'. The rabbi didn't open the door. The disciple knocked again and the rabbi repeated his question. The disciple once again answered: 'It is I, master.' Again, silence. After going through this several times, the disciple heard the rabbi ask 'Who is it?' yet again and decided to say nothing. Only then did the rabbi open the door and make the following observation: 'Every time you answered using the word 'I', there was no one outside, only illusion. For none but the Eternal One can use the word 'I' without it being an illusion.'*

Then how are we to achieve a real sense of who we are?

In the Jewish tradition, the morning liturgy asks: 'What are we? What is our life? What is our power? What is our strength? What is our justice? What is our compassion? Nothing! But nonetheless, 'who are we?' We are Your creatures!'

When asked in reference to 'I,' the question 'what' really means 'nothing.' What are we? Nothing, as the rabbi told the disciple who said 'I.' But if the question is properly reframed and we ask 'who are we?' instead of 'what are we?', then 'I' gains meaning. This 'I' represents a relationship (whom) rather than an essence (what). This is the most basic sense of self. We are in relation to others; we are in relation to a Creator.

No intelligence based on essence (on what) will produce reverence but only illusion. And in the final analysis, illusion is what gives birth to inefficiency. Only if you develop a sense of self based on your relationships with others will you produce reverences for yourself. Our parents, our children, our friends, our lovers, our opponents, and nature form the raw material of 'who we are.'

Realize that the only face you will never know is your own. We may know ourselves from our reflection in a mirror, from photographs, or even from TV screens. But never will we see ourselves face to face. And if this doesn't seem to matter much, think a little about what it would be like to know someone—your father or mother, for example—only through reflections, photographs, or screens. It is obvious they wouldn't have the 'life' that a face-to-face encounter brings us.

Because we are undifferentiated from our surroundings—since we cannot see ourselves—our sense of self has no meaning as an essence, as 'what.' It is reflected in our mother's eyes that we first see ourselves. It is reflected in the eyes of all the people with whom we relate that we gain a true sense of self, of 'who' we are in relation to those who hold our reflection.

Sense of Purpose

Replacing 'Why?' with 'Why not?'

This sense is very often misunderstood within the realm of spirituality. The sense of purpose that seeks to bring order to the world around us is constantly bombarded by situations of disorder. Any attempt to generate purpose is a result of our desire to control. I remember something that happened to me when I went to visit a patient at a hospital specialized in catastrophic illnesses. The person's illness had gone into remission, and while I was there he received the news he would be released. I had the opportunity to hug him and share in his joy. I left his room with a very special feeling that there is purpose in our lives, that someone is watching out over the world. However, as I stepped out of his room, I found myself in a hallway lined with doors into countless other rooms, each holding its own reality.

The order that I wanted to create, that was my concern at that moment, does not exist. If it did exist, all those who had not received the blessing of a cure would have to exist outside of this reality. We cannot change what happens to us. We have no control over what happens to us. What we do control and what we can change is what we do about what happens to us.

The greatest source of our suffering lies in trying to understand 'why?'

Like a bed sheet that is too short, the 'why's' always end up leaving a part of reality uncovered, in the effort to cover up another part.

If we are to perceive things in a way that does not disguise reality, it is essential that we accept the fact that things can happen to us and that life must be lived from the perspective of 'why not?' 'Why not?' is not an expression of complacency or an attitude meant to sweep aside emotions of anger. Much to the contrary, 'why not?' reflects a healthy, emotional maturation of such feelings of anger. Because it means we have reached the point where our frustrations and pain merely hurt. Whoever can experience the question 'why not?' can feel pain but does not suffer from the effort to keep this pain from being felt again. Pain arises from an unpleasant situation but it is about more than that. Pain is a sense that reveals reality. It points us to both physical and emotional troubles and reflects points of encounter between our existence and reality. On the one hand, pain allows us to make corrections that 'cure' or minimize our discomfort, but perhaps this is not its purpose. Just as our eyes were made so we can see what we want and also what we don't want, we can demand nothing different from pain. If we expect the sense produced by pain to be only functional (to feel good) and not a measure of our relationship with the world, then this is the same as asking ourselves: 'Why should I have eyes if it is to see what I'm seeing?'

A well-known Chinese parable illustrates this sense:

> *A man had a handsome horse that was the envy of the whole village. Someone offered him a good price for the beast, but he turned down the offer. A few days later, his horse escaped and ran away. His neighbors told him: 'You should have sold him!' To which the man replied: 'Maybe yes, maybe no.'*
>
> *One night the horse came back, and since it had become the leader of a wild herd, it brought along a couple dozen other horses. The man's neighbors said: 'It's a good thing you didn't sell him!' To which the man replied: 'Maybe yes, maybe no.'*
>
> *One fine day, the man's son went to mount the horse. He fell, broke his hip, and had to spend six months flat on his back. The man's neighbors said: 'You should have sold him!' To which the man came back: 'Maybe yes, maybe no!'*
>
> *A war broke out in the region and all young men were drafted, except for this fellow's son, who was still laid up recovering from his fractures. Few were those who escaped the bloody war with their lives and fewer still those who suffered no permanent injury. The man's*

neighbors said: 'It's a good thing you didn't sell the horse!' To which the man replied: 'Maybe yes, maybe no.'

Whenever we try to interpret our world from the perspective of 'why?', we freeze the process of life. The answer that we may find at one moment will dissolve in another, for life is dynamic and constantly changes perspectives. When we are able to perceive the question 'why not?', we are open to the possibilities contained in the man's answer of 'maybe yes, maybe no.'

All the man did was decide not to sell his horse. The idea that there is a right decision—one that will eventually, when all is said and done, prove to have been the most advantageous—is part of an illusion and of our desire to achieve control.

'Why not?' frees us from a fate determined by the mistakes and successes of our past and allows the present to determine our experience.

'Why not?' is not about having no purpose; it is instead spiritual purpose itself—the purpose of shadow and not of light. Its advantage is that it frees us to struggle for the present and for the future, rather than making us lose ourselves in inaction while we endeavor to 'understand' our past.

Sense of Confidence

The idea of 'up above'

An inner sense of 'why not?' can only be developed if it is accompanied by a deep sense of confidence.

And confidence is not a human rationalization but a basic sentiment. Our hunger is satisfied by the maternal breast, revealing to us one of the universe's deep secrets: there is a concern corresponding to every need. In point of fact, need itself is part of a process that seeks to satisfy this need. Our need might not be satisfied in certain context but we recognize an order implicit to every living thing based on the fact that needs only exist when and if they can be satisfied. No living process is built on the basis of impossibilities. When a child feels hungry for the first time, it cannot imagine the incredible resource available to it—the maternal breast, designed to meet its needs. The existence of this breast is proof of 'order'. Even for those who never have their hunger satiated by this breast, it exists.

Our sense of confidence develops out of this piece of reality. It comes together with expectation and hope, which in themselves reflect a high degree of order. There is a Hasidic story that describes the attitude towards life of someone with confidence, someone who trusts.

It demonstrates not only intelligence but its magic efficiency as well:

During Russia's frigid winter, the rabbi continued to take his ritual baths in an almost frozen river. His disciples couldn't understand how a man of his age could stand such icy waters. So they decided to give it a try themselves and see how they would fare. To their surprise, the biggest challenge wasn't the temperature of the water but getting out. The steep frozen banks were almost impossible to scale. The disciples would slip back and only with great effort, by helping each other, did they manage to climb back out. Filled with curiosity, they rushed to the rabbi.

'Rabbi, now we know how hard it is to enter the icy waters, but how do you manage to climb the frozen, slippery banks?'

The rabbi explained to them: 'The secret, my dears, is always having something to grab onto up above.'

'Up above' is the place of order. 'Above' and 'below' define our basic perception of order. When we feel unprotected, we feel like a motherless child. Or when we feel we've been treated unfairly, we want to know 'Who's the manager? Who's the boss around here?' We look for support from up above. Neither justice nor security will necessarily be attained from what lies above us, but knowing that it exists, that it is real, and that it is a concrete possibility is a correct (and therefore efficacious) interpretation of reality.

Without developing this sense, it becomes very tough to climb over certain walls in life. Life around us provides us with such a low friction coefficient that it's hard to stay on our feet without this help from above—without this sense of confidence.

It is important to recognize that 'up above' does not mean you will always have your needs met by the saving breast that comes from above. Much to the contrary, confidence comes not only from the experience of knowing this breast, but primarily from its absence. The need which expresses itself in tears and complaints but which does not lose sight of the fact that there is something to believe in, something to hope for, will always have before it the possibility of that which comes from above.

The story goes that a rabbi once joined a crowd that was admiring the stunts of a tight-rope walker at a circus. His disciples were surprised to find the rabbi engaged in such a worldly pastime, and so they asked him about it. The rabbi then inquired of them:

'Do you know how he does it?' And without waiting for an answer, he went on.

'Rule number one: never let your attention be distracted by the hat where people are tossing money in appreciation of the show. If you lose your concentration, you'll fall right away.

'Rule number two: don't pay attention to your next step but keep your eyes on the pole at the end of the rope. The goal is what makes balance possible and provides the stability needed to take the next step. But what is the hardest and most important moment in his task?'

The disciples looked at each other in perplexity.

He answered: 'It's when he reaches the end of the rope and has to turn around, and he does not have the pole as a reference point. He depends upon a center that he has internalized.'

We can extract some important lessons from this quasi manual of procedures. Don't look just for immediate reward, or you will lose your balance. Don't forget to have a goal to focus on, or you will also lose your balance. But what matters most of all is acquiring confidence and internalizing an external reference point, so that you can persevere even when it is not there.

Like the maternal breast that lends us confidence, like all situations in which life satisfies our needs—for air, space, warmth, pressure, etc.— we should learn to internalize this breast so that it will serve as a marker of confidence whenever it is not there.

At such times of trouble in our lives—when we don't seem to have any reference to rely on, any pole to guide us, any tangible hope—our sense of confidence becomes our indispensable center.

This kind of intelligence is incredibly efficacious when it comes to dealing with death itself and perhaps, more importantly yet, when it comes to not fearing death through our lives. Whoever manages to combine the sense of 'why not?' with the sense of 'up above' will have achieved something as powerful as immortality: freedom from the fear of dying.

Sense of Passage

If not now, when?

One of the greatest obstacles to intelligence is our desire for routine. Routine is the mechanism we use to conceal from ourselves one of the most important senses we have: the sense of passage. Routine's prime objective is predictability and control. And all of us—some more, others less—resort to this trick in order to avoid the pain our egos suffer because we know our lives to be transitory.

It's not at all unusual for an elderly person to become very upset when he notices one particular object out of place. This object opens the door to a vital of reality: unpredictability. The object that is out of place is the tomorrow that might not come. Our date books, our travel plans, and our projects are imbued with the feeling that what we will be doing in two, four, or seven years is guaranteed. But it is quite possible that these future years will not exist. The condition of the future, even the future nearest at hand—tomorrow or the next moment—is inexistence.

This distorted interpretation of reality can have an enormous impact on our quality of life. All of our priorities can be altered by a false supposition regarding how much time we have. No strategy can be even minimally efficacious if its understanding of time limits and deadlines is totally wrong. Such strategies based on false maps of reality are what cause us so much anxiety and unrest. We know we aren't ready to go, we have the feeling we're not prepared to leave this world in the next second, and our ensuing impotence leaves us angry and afraid.

But what does 'being ready to go' mean? This circumstance is quite extraordinary and simple at the same time. Being ready to leave this world means living by the sage Hillel's maxim: 'If not now, when?' This attitude towards life does not imply a now-only attitude, one incapable of building and investing. Much to the contrary, it implies a correct reading of reality: tomorrow may never come, but most likely it will. And so we have a sense of passage and not of finitude. After all, the notion of end is only pertinent for those who do not *live* the passage. And it is only when we value the present that this passage is experienced as the greatest gift of existence.

When we experience the present and all of its potential, we gain a feeling of well-being enjoyed by those who do not live in fear of finitude and its unfairness. This is because whoever lives the present as his or her final moment has no reason to constantly record the 'unfairnesses' of reality.

The examination of our routine as a trick that causes us tremendous emotional damage is a task falling to psychoanalytical therapies, based on the sense of spirituality expressed in the notion of passage.

A Chinese tale serves as a good example of this sense:

It is said that an emperor decided to have a spectacular garden planted. As part of its inauguration, he wanted to order a plaque inscribed with very special sayings. He summoned the most respected thinkers of his kingdom to dispute the task, and the wisest was commissioned to write the happiest, most positive sentence he could create.

The wise man thought for months before coming up with words that would be notable and positive enough. When the emperor unveiled the plaque, he saw this inscription: 'The grandfather died; the father died; the son died.' The emperor was infuriated. After all, he had requested something happy and upbeat. What did this wise man mean by offering him a list of dead men?

Incensed, the emperor demanded to know: 'What is the meaning of this?'

The sage replied: 'There is nothing neither happier nor more extraordinary than when things happen in due time.'

There is nothing sadder than the reversal of this 'order', which is reality's most likely result (thanks to God or to order), yet still not a guaranteed result. And that is what the wise man meant to say: this is the greatest happiness—the utmost order, for which we are grateful. Life can always be lived happily, even when our expectations regarding this order are frustrated, as long as we live a healthy measure of 'if not now, when?' What the wise man offers the emperor is the supreme situation, the most extraordinary one possible. And is there any alternative better than each passing generation having a full life? No.

The most valuable lesson in this story is that it demonstrates the most 'well-ordered' scenario for us human beings while nevertheless demonstrating that our lives are transitory.

It is only this feeling -- this sense of passage -- that can free individuals from the yoke of that which is to come. And it is this freedom that we perceive as well-being. The future is not a dream but a nightmare if in its name we renounce the power of the present. Every time the word 'when' is used in reference to something essential in our lives, there is only one answer: 'Now!'

Sense of Limits

Because it is so

The sense of passage produces another sense: reverence for limits. Recognizing limits is one important expression of intelligence. We often believe that this sense develops out of rules of logic which enable us to calculate risks. Yet a limit is only given by a true limit, such as our passage.

When it comes to money, the logic goes: 'How much money would be enough? And the answer is: just a little bit more.' Limits have to be found in another structure of reasoning. And this has to do with discernment achieved by the process of starting from the end and moving towards the beginning, if we are to encounter any form of intelligence. Based on this concept, an ancient practice employed by scribes and calligraphers would start writing from the end of a line backwards once it reached the middle of that line. Since he had to fit a certain number of words for each line in the space available, the scribe had to make use of this technique. This was the only way he could perceive the true limits within which he was operating and thereby achieve the desired aesthetic effect. Eyes that see limits will automatically tend towards more intelligent ways of behavior. The same is true of our existential issues. As soon as we gain consciousness that our lives are transitory—even if we don't know their exact duration—we endeavor to adopt attitudes that take this reality into account in a more precise, all-encompassing fashion, and the result is both efficiency and well-being.

The notion of limits can be perceived as a measure of sensitivity if we analyze this simple mathematical equation: Who is richer: someone who has 100 units of money or someone who has 200? If we use logic but do not take the notion of limits into account, the obvious answer is the person with 200 units. However, if the person with 100 units wants to accumulate 150, and the one with 200 wants to accumulate 400, then the former is richer—that is, closer to his goal—since he only needs another 50 units while the latter needs another 200.

If we take limits into account, we see a different reality. And when we understand that the notion of limits changes our perception of reality, we are able to interpret reality much more accurately. Therefore, just as important as obtaining objective data about reality is our ability to recognize boundaries and frames.

A wonderful story handed down through Jewish tradition demonstrates this in the existential realm:

> *In a small town, the local rabbi dreamt that on a given day and at a given time, all the dead in the city would rise up for exactly one half hour.*
>
> *All the families in town were thrilled. Although skeptical about the rabbi's prediction, their desire to be re-united with their loved ones was so great that they crowded about the cemetery gate, waiting for the appointed hour.*
>
> *They were tremendously excited. The idea of seeing their loved ones again electrified the entire village. They thought: and what to do with just half an hour with our loved ones? Some got ready to hug and kiss their relatives the whole time. Others prepared huge feasts and gathered all their kinfolk to spend the time together. Some had issues to deal with—quarrels that needed settling, apologies to make, or information that had been carried to the grave and that the living wanted to know.*
>
> *At the exact moment foretold by the rabbi, an amazing thing happened. The graves began to open and the spirits stood up. But to everyone's surprise, instead of throwing themselves into the arms of their loved ones, the spirits set off in a mad dash.*
>
> *The throng of family and friends anxiously waiting to exchange displays of affection couldn't believe their eyes. Their own relatives*

didn't stop to pay the slightest attention to them but simply ran off, all in the same direction. So they followed to see where they were going.

The spirits were headed no place other than the House of Studies— the synagogue—where the community's books were kept. They yanked books off the shelves and devoured them with amazing enthusiasm.

When the thirty minutes were up, they all rushed back to the cemetery and one by one climbed into their tombs and returned to their eternal rest.

Why did they behave this way? Perhaps because the most important thing in our lives is not one more hug from our loved ones—for this is an expression of attachment. The spirits' desire was to reach for perfection. Their half hour afforded them a chance to seek the most precious thing that exists in our world: inner values. The outer world is the world of passage, and they didn't want to waste their time trying to master or control it. Of course their studies were not simply meant to obtain information or achieve some practical end; they wanted to fill in gaps that had been left by the limitations of their inner education.

Half an hour of catharses or of seeking growth that had been feared earlier—this was the option made by those who knew the essence of limits. The dead (now more alive than the living) understood the essence of life to be a measure of internal rather than of external experience.

When children reach the phase of asking 'why' all the time, they are testing the limits of reality. Their seemingly endless chains of 'why's' lead parents from explanation to explanation until every parent, without exception, ends up declaring 'because!' This 'because' teaches a valuable lesson about limits. It is 'because' that allows us—like scribes—to start writing from the end to the beginning. And so it is thanks to 'because' that there is never an interruption in the flow nor a lack of aesthetics in what happens in reality.

Sense of Direction

Replacing 'Where to?' with 'Where from?'

Just as we need an intelligence that provides us with a sense of 'up above,' it is also essential for us to develop a sense of 'where to.' Once again, like all other senses, this one is not derived from a strategy or a desire. It instead becomes apparent through our experience and through the relationships we establish between our inner and outer worlds. Living is always the art of trying to satisfy our inner desires and needs while relying on the possibilities and resources available in our outer worlds. In other words, while our journey is external, our rudder is internal. It is the rudder that keeps us headed in the direction we choose.

> *A man once decided to fast from the close of one Saturday until the next. He disciplined himself strictly, and come Friday he was still fulfilling his promise.*
>
> *But around noon that day, his thirst grew unbearable. He thought he would die if he didn't give in, and so he went to a spring to quench his thirst. But just as he was about to drink, he thought to himself: 'I've already waited so long…to fall short of my goal by just a few hours…' He immediately turned away from the spring and managed to get his thirst under control. But then he was hit by another thought: 'Not drinking some water just because there are a few hours left doesn't make a bit of sense. This wasn't the reason I decided to fast, as if it*

were a kind of contest. Drinking would be better than the hypocrisy of holding out for a few more hours!'

So he went back to the spring, ready to drink, with the idea that this would be the most commendable action under his circumstances. But to his surprise, as he approached the spring he discovered he was no longer thirsty.

When night fell and the holy Sabbath arrived, the man went to pray with the rabbi, his revered master. The rabbi, however, treated him with disdain the whole night. When the man was about to leave, the master called him over and said: 'Your soul is like a patchwork quilt!'

Why would the rabbi so harshly reprimand someone who apparently was struggling against his own hypocrisy? After all, the man in the story was able to remain aware that his choices were made solely in response to external values. He had been able to renounce the vanity underlying his desire to 'succeed' when he realized that his task has turned from an internal act to an external one. And it might be indeed because of his keen sensitivity that the rabbi reprimands him. For it is the task of a rabbi to know a 'trick' when he sees one.

Tricks are rational (external) attempts to cope with internal tensions. Of course they will not work, or they will work only temporarily. They are not only inefficacious; tricks also distance us further from our resolutions because they disguise our situation and keep tensions from appearing in all their clarity. They are like certain drugs that offer momentary relief but that cover up the underlying problem and hamper diagnoses.

The rabbi knows that the man's story is more complex than the story of someone who simply fails to keep a vow. A person who eats in hiding manages to fool others, but this particular fellow not only fooled others but—worse yet—fooled himself as well. Because he lost touch with inner meaning, even though he relied on the noblest values available to him, he was lost. This is the patchwork quilt the rabbi was talking about. The man is made up of so many patches of himself that he gets lost in an inner maze of confused desires and indecision. All the attitudes he takes—even the noblest ones, as when he tries not to be a hypocrite, for example—are merely tricks meant to produce a counterpane fashioned from a single piece of cloth, one that will replace the patchwork quilt.

But this is only possible if we have our own inner direction. Such a covering can never be made of appearances or scenarios that serve only to fool others or, worse, ourselves.

Our success and what we make of our lives are directly linked to this sense of direction, to what we want as our counterpane.

> *A rabbi once discovered that the richest millionaire in his town had given an incredible donation to a rabbi in another town, in support of the local House of Studies. The rabbi thought to himself: 'If he gave such a huge amount of money to the House of Studies in another city... imagine what he has in mind for our House of Studies, in his own town?' So the rabbi went to talk to the millionaire, who received him most cordially.*
>
> *The rabbi talked about his work and about the wonderful educational and social projects under his auspices, and the rich man offered to help as he could. He pulled out his checkbook, wrote out a check, and handed it to the rabbi. When the rabbi saw the amount, he couldn't believe his eyes. It was a tenth of what the millionaire had given the other rabbi.*
>
> *As he was leaving, the rabbi, who could no longer hide his disappointment, summoned the courage to say: 'Please excuse me, sir, but I heard that the House of Studies in the next town received a much larger donation than what you've given ours. Why the difference— especially since this is your home town?'*
>
> *The millionaire was surprised. He thought for a while and then said: 'I hadn't stopped to think about it but now that you ask, I think I can explain. The other rabbi came to visit me on a very rainy day. He got here with his shoes covered in mud and when he came in, he walked across my white Persian carpet without giving it a thought. Then he sat down in his dripping wet raincoat on my couch—imported from France—and he didn't even take a glance at my collection of art objects and paintings. He made me feel as if all these things were worthless. So when I wrote out the check, I wrote it for a huge sum, because it didn't seem worth very much to me.'*
>
> *'But when you stepped into my house, I noticed you paid a great deal of attention to the things of value here. I could see how much you were impressed by them, and when you asked me for a contribution,*

everything seemed so valuable to me that I couldn't imagine giving you any more than what I did.'

The rabbi from the other town was not a 'patchwork quilt'. His intentions were not external but internal. It must be understood that the notion of 'internal' has nothing to do with having a non-personal interest. No doubt there is something personal about every counterpane but integrity and honesty are internal in nature. This rabbi's counterpane was not made of patches so that reality could be manipulated to fit into it, artificially. His desire was only one and not a ragtag combination of different desires, arranged so they appeared to have one meaning, to be made from one piece of cloth.

Not yielding to the trick of thinking that we can have greater control over reality from the outside is what preserves our sense of direction.

The dilemma of the messenger who forgets the delivery address is not as serious as the dilemma of the messenger who forgets not only the delivery address but also the contents of the message itself. The notion of a patchwork quilt addresses the dilemma of the messenger who forgets not only the address and the content but doesn't know who sent the message either.

Our sense of direction depends upon our maintaining a clear notion of who the sender is.

Sense of Discerning

Knowing before you know

In Jewish tradition, the morning prayers begin with a strange blessing that recognizes the grandeur of the Creator for endowing the rooster with the ability to discern the difference between day and night.

Why are such praises sung to this talent of the rooster? What makes this ability so remarkable that it actually represents a form of spiritual intelligence?

The rooster's ability is special not because he discerns the beginning of day, when the sky starts to lighten, but because he is able to detect the moment when nighttime ceases, before daytime has even yet begun. Herein lies his merit: he manages to know before he even knows. But what does he know?

What the rooster discerns—the difference between night and day—is the greatest symbol of the human relationship to life. 'Night' is always an allusion to the darkness of despair and exile. 'Day', on the other hand, is an allusion to the clarity of hope and recovery.

It is interesting to note that Biblical tradition identifies in King David this specific talent to discern. As legend goes, King David would awake 'in the middle of the night,' at the moment when the first part of nighttime was ending. According to Jewish tradition, nighttime commences at sunset and grows in strength until 'the middle of the night.' From then on, its strength dwindles until the day reaches a point of 'saturation', causing nighttime to turn into daytime. It is this moment that the rooster is sensitive enough to discern.

The Psalms stand as a classic model of writings produced by spiritual intelligence. And King David, their author, is a prime example of someone with a high quotient of spiritual intelligence. He is not like his son, King Solomon, the archetypical figure of the wise man, endowed with a wisdom that uses both logic and emotion. In this regard, David is less wise; however, he was endowed with a remarkable sense of discerning.

In his episode with Goliath, it was David's ability to discern, to believe in something no one else believed in, that rendered his actions efficacious and made him victorious. His success derived from his faith-driven determination and his ability to see light in the midst of darkness, because he knew night was already ending.

According to legend, David woke up exactly in the middle of the night, when it was losing its potency and had begun its retreat. This nighttime moment—which is already the beginning of daytime, even in total darkness—is an incredibly rich time. We can see this in our own lives, for the moment when darkness disappears is of much greater impact than light itself. And we can all remember times when things seemed to be going badly, and then to our great surprise, everything turned out fine. More remarkable yet is when we perceive the exact moment when darkness gives way to clarity, precisely before light has yet arrived.

This is why the Psalms are the favorite reading material of people facing major challenges in their lives. Whether the circumstances involve illness, mourning, or depression, the Psalms are more efficacious than any other text exactly because they provide hope which lies not in light but in darkness that has lost its strength. No one who is going through such trials will find inspiration in light, or in the notion that 'everything will be fine,' since this person's concrete situation will be surrounded by shadow and uncertainty. What is profoundly sensitive about the Psalms is that they offer solace without resorting to promises that 'everything is or will be fine.' This kind of 'light' clouds things for those who are struggling with limits and doubts. The Psalms are singular because they are a literary product created 'in the middle of the night,' when all is still dark but the mandate has already been given for light to come.

The Psalms restore a sense of well-being without resorting to trite promises of redemption or resolution but rather by delineating ways out. Their task is to show that night has turned the corner and day shines ahead—just as a night of insomnia and restlessness finds the kiss of hope and gives way to sweet sleep near the break of day.

In other words, spiritual intelligence means foreseeing sweetness in the midst of bitterness, growth in the midst of suffering, or feeling ground beneath our feet even when we have been driven from our land.

To develop this form of intelligence, we need the various senses we are examining here, especially the sense of discerning, which grows out of our relationship with darkness. As part of this process, we must understand that the dark holds rich deposits of life, deposits not found in the light. Repeating this idea: complete light cannot reproduce the existential richness found in implicit light, at the moment when night turns the corner towards dawn. This hidden light is the raw material not only of hope but also of spiritual intelligence.

> *A man once got lost in a forest. He tried as best he could to find his way out but he failed. As night fell, he was growing desperate. Suddenly he spotted a light in the distance. He soon saw that it was a man holding aloft a lantern. He was overjoyed, certain his troubles were over. He approached the fellow and said: 'I was lost, but thank heavens I found you!' The man holding the lantern replied with a voice filled with pity: 'I'm very sorry... I'm lost too! But don't despair. You know where you've looked for a way out, and I know where I've looked. Together we have a much better chance of finding it.'*
>
> *While the first man was trying to console himself, he noticed that the man with the lantern had his eyes closed. He cried out: 'Are you blind?!' 'Yes,' the other replied. 'So why do you need a lantern?' 'Well, the lantern's not for me. It's not so I can see, but so others can see me.'*

As we travel through life, our resources are not limited solely to 'light', that is, to that which gives us pleasure or allows us to build things. We can avail ourselves of another group of resources, which come from the dark, from blindness. Not from a resigned blindness but from blindness that holds a lantern. I am talking about all light that we cannot use to see, about hidden light—the light that does not turn night into day but that breaks the back of darkness and instills in us the hope that we will discover the means of finding our way out of the forest. Our suffering alone does not enable us to see but it prompts us to ignite the lanterns of meeting. We discover that the other and our relationships with others are essential resources in our struggle to make our way through the forest's infinite pathways.

It is this infinity that leaves us feeling like we're lost. Our way actually lies in the lanterns that help us see and also in the lanterns that make us visible. As these lanterns shine their light and occasion encounters, they undo the impression that we are lost. The way out is not a way out but a different way of being.

All spiritual intelligence involves the ability to re-contextualize our despair and to learn to make darkness a less inhospitable place. To this end, we must renounce any expectation of seeing but instead relish the joy of the broken dark, of the dying night.

Sense of a Way Out

In search of the same that is different

Our intelligence can only take advantage of the darkness if we are able to discern its redeeming potential. The rooster does not represent merely the moment which inaugurates night's defeat. Its intelligence symbolizes the understanding that the very nature of nighttime is to lead into daytime, since both are one and the same phenomenon. The rooster's cry to the world, announcing the approaching morning, carries the revelation that darkness is not a foe of life. Darkness itself holds a unique understanding of daytime—an understanding that not even the light of morning can achieve.

To find our way out of the forest, we should not seek refuge somewhere outside, disconnected from the place that frightens us. The blind man in last chapter's story symbolizes the difference between the concept of fleeing and the concept of integrating things, of bringing them into unity. The man is able to deliver his message of serenity because he lives with darkness. He knows that by integrating what he sees with what he doesn't see he will find the mysterious way out that allows him to remain in the same place in a different way. That's why we find desperate, lost people in the same place where we find peaceful people basking in contentedness. How can people be so different in the same place?

A time-honored Sufi story tells of a man who was crouched on the ground looking for something, when along came a friend. Seeing what the fellow was doing, his friend asked: 'Did you happen to lose something?'

'Yes…I lost a key and I can't find it.

The friend at once set about helping in the search. After feeling around and exploring a large area, the friend asked in frustration: 'Are you sure you lost the key here?'

'Here? No…no, I didn't lose it here… I lost it…there!' the fellow replied, pointing to a spot farther away.

Indignant, the friend complained: 'Are you nuts? If you lost it over there, why are you looking here?'

'Oh, well, because it's light over here and I can see. Over there it's awfully dark!'

This is not an unusual portrait of our lives. Not rarely do we find ourselves searching for keys in places where there is light. But the keys aren't there. As hard as we might look, we will never find them, for they lie in impossibly dark places where we would never dare venture.

We become upset at the cruelty of life whenever we undertake a sincere and persistent search that leads to nothing. We blame the heavens when we can't find keys at the right time, and we call order into question. In point of fact, many people confuse faith, hope, and optimism with an ability to search with greater determination. These people tell themselves: 'If I haven't found it, it's because I didn't try hard enough.' But this is just our way of avoiding dark places replete with keys.

Spiritual intelligence tears us away from the place where there is light and, despite all ensuing hardships, leads us into darkness. The rooster's role is to teach and show us, through our experiences in life and in the hours before dawn, that there is a redemptive darkness. King David, whose holy insomnia kept him from missing these magic moments when the purest light can be seen in the midst of darkness, is another model, taken from the Psalms. This book of the Bible endeavors to convey something that cannot be taught in the form of a manual or instructions. Its goal is to give us the incomparable experience of finding keys where we'd rather not look. These experiences are what evolve into spiritual intelligence.

Whenever we witness someone trying to account for a complicated life experience by following the path of light, we should suspect them of trying to look for keys where there are none. This is why religions, and even spirituality, so easily fall prey to futile quests where there is light. The excessive number of 'theologies' and explanations that behave like 24-hour spotlights to illuminate our searches is one of the most insidious traps. These ways of experiencing religion and spirituality make us spiritually stupid. They are sophisticated forms of alienation, and at times they gain institutional status with the sole purpose of 'exorcising' darkness. The Devil is placed on one side and God on the other, and the hunt is on—yet only where there is light. But this proposal that life be free from fear, that we never need venture into the dark to search for keys, is terror itself, the true devil.

As time goes by, the shadows gain strength. Places of light are reduced to islands under the ever greater threat of darkness. Panic and spiritual phobias set in and there are fewer and fewer ways out. Showered by keys they will never discover, such people are like prisoners, until they move to bring darkness back to their lives. As the saying goes: Religion is for those who are afraid of Hell; true spirituality is for those who have already been there.

Every experience that resembles the rooster's crowing—where we discern redemption and change in the midst of darkness—teaches us to invest harder in the quest for more experiences of the same sort. With each experience where we find the way out in the same place—our place of imprisonment—we grow more spiritually refined.

When we think the way out is to end our marriage, change jobs, move cities, find new friends, acquire new interests, and so on, we are looking for another place of light where we can pretend keys will be found. Whenever we can no longer fool ourselves into thinking the keys we need are to be found in a place of light, we feel the need to temporarily find another refuge for our illusions. The keys that once lay in places of light were all found long ago. The ones we're really looking for, the ones that seem so hard for us to find, are certainly not there.

Looking at a marriage, a job, a friend, or a city from the perspective of darkness means looking at things that will not make us leave the place where we are imprisoned, even if we change them a thousand times. And looking at these situations from the perspective of darkness also means looking at them from the perspective that frightens us.

Out of this darkness that liberates—more than light itself—comes spirituality.

Learning to seek dark places and training ourselves to want this darkness are the tough yet noble tasks of spiritual growth. The spirits who rose from the dead for half an hour understood this. Coming from the shadows and no longer fearing them, they used their second chance at life to try to run to the dark places and their hidden keys. They didn't want the light of attachment, even when that represented the affection of their loved ones. They did not want the light of pretending they were not alone, independent and separate from the reality of the other.

In such places—which can be any place, or the same place—there is a way out. We only need to see them differently, look at them from the angle that appears obscure to us and reject the fatal vice of turning on the lights. The monsters disappear in the light but so too does the possibility of finding ways out that we will some day need. Instead of turning on the lights, the idea is to approach darkness and realize exactly when the nighttime begins to come undone, even in the middle of it. We must become like David, who received his monsters not with hymns to light but with hymns to the hidden light of night. In search of the same that is different.

Sense of Reconciliation

Transforming fear into action

What is darkness?

When we come into this world and discover there are ways to satisfy all of our desires, we learn about the concept of order. The air we breathe, the maternal breast, and the affection we receive all unveil a world that leads us spiritually to 'Santa Claus.' This is the best children's definition of God—the being who is responsible for satisfying our desires. This is the God of gifts and the magic of pleasure, which seems infinite and unrestricted. But Santa Claus doesn't exist, at least not in this childish sense.

For many, this dramatic discovery scraps forestalls any need to invest in spiritual intelligence. Yet this should be only the first stage of spiritual development. When we discover that needs which could be satisfied sometimes aren't, we should embark on a desperate search for meaning. If our needs and expectations have not been met, should we take it as something personal? Is it possible that we don't deserve to have them fulfilled? Is it possible we aren't as loved as we had thought? What must we do to please the cosmos and once again enjoy its protection?

In part, darkness is formed from those experiences when our needs are not satisfied, which bring us in touch with the notion of death and injustice. But it is not the simple fact that our desires are not realized that constitutes darkness. We human beings have been endowed with the resources to wrestle with a problem or flee from it. Both attitudes can save us. When faced with a certain situation or dilemma, if we decide not to stand up to the challenge, we automatically flee from it—and visa versa. If we face the problem successfully, we are saved—and we experience the feeling that God is on our side, watching out for us. Likewise, if we flee successfully—so long as this flight represents a conscious strategy—we have effectively wrestled with our problem and we will experience the same feeling. However, if we fail in our effort to face a challenge—in other words, if we end up forced to flee—or if fleeing is not a strategic choice, we are left humiliated and frightened. This God (this order) is a god who abandons us, who allows us to taste the bitterness of defeat and feel insecure about our very survival.

Darkness is the product of a paradox Job describes in the form of an equation: 'When I fight successfully or flee courageously, God loves me. When I fail or flee in cowardice, either God doesn't love me—or there's something wrong with my concept of God.'

Spiritual intelligence requires us to reconcile two contradictory situations: we must recognize that when we are successful in facing a problem or in fleeing from it, this means that order is protecting us; at the same time, when we face a challenge but fail in our effort or when we flee in cowardly fashion, this doesn't mean we've lost this protection or it doesn't exist. Whether you are a rational thinker or a believer, this is an unbearable paradox. Rational thinkers will argue that it isn't a paradox but a contradiction. Believers will try to camouflage the failure by reversing it into some kind of hidden success that will be revealed at a later moment or in another world. The problem with both kinds of people is that they are operating in places where there is light. And what is important about paradoxes is precisely that they represent places of dark.

Darkness therefore does not represent evil. It is simply a place where things aren't seen clearly, like a paradox.

We are surrounded by such paradoxes. If you want to live well, you must have a great deal of drive and attachment so you can fight for what you want. But at the same time, and paradoxically, you must live ready for the possibility that you will die in a moment and have to give everything up. If either of the two sides of this 'paradox' is missing, the tension that constitutes well-being will be gone. Although this appears to be a very dark place, through refinement or spiritual intelligence we learn to no longer regard it as frightening. To the contrary, this place uncovers an imperceptible light, a dawn that the rooster knows—and that is more filled with hope than light itself.

The place of light is a place that holds no contradictory feelings or experiences. Darkness, on the other hand, is not the place of evil but a place that mixes feelings and perceptions. Anxiety is an example of this mixture. It is a feeling that contains both love and hate. The reconciliation of these sentiments results in a dark place from which we want to distance ourselves, even though important keys lie there. Doubt is another example. It embraces two desires, or two rights, or two wrongs, or two benefits, or two costs.

Neither anxieties nor doubts vanish when the lights are turned on. It is only in this place where sentiments and perceptions are mixed that the hidden light of darkness can be found. If we know how to remain in these dark places—in an effort to absorb their teachings—instead of running away from them, we will be investing in spiritual intelligence. Quite to the contrary of what many religious proposals preach, spiritual intelligence has little to do with certainty but rather with the reconciliation of seemingly contradictory poles. Everything born from anything that goes against or counter something else—like *en-counters*—but which results in a paradoxical reconciliation is spiritual.

It is said that a student of Abraham Joshua Heschel once declared indignantly that a statement made by his teacher was a paradox, and the theologian replied: 'Yes, it's just a paradox!' A paradox is not a dead-end or a mistake—it's just a paradox. Spirituality is the area of human intelligence capable of dealing with paradoxes and contradictions. It wouldn't constitute a form of intelligence if there were no way to travel through such deep darkness with some measure of cognition or reference. These reference points are the senses and reverences we develop throughout our lives. And these senses are what reconcile and sustain a way in which—in the form of darkness—we can see and discern things, despite the lack of light, certainty, or definition.

A spiritualized person is someone who knows how to walk in the shadows, as we are told in Psalm 23, verse 4: '*Yea though I walk through the valley of the shadow of death, I will fear no evil.*' This doesn't mean we're talking about someone morbid or depressed but someone who reconciles contradictory feelings and understandings and who does not fear—unlike people who live in light, who are stranded in light, people who are beings of fear and terror.

This is a basic rule: *the more you turn the lights on, the greater your fear of the dark.* Control is nothing but a way of damming up fear. Fear—the material from which shadow is formed—is also the means that allows us to see hidden light. Whenever we reconcile contradictory feelings and perceptions, fear is automatically transformed into action. Contrary to what we usually think, true fear does not paralyze us but moves us to action. It urges us to face things and not run away.

According to the Baal Shem Tov: *'In worldly matters, there can be no fear where there is happiness, and neither can there be happiness where there is fear. But when it comes to that which is holy, where there is fear one always finds joy, and visa versa.'* This 'fear' is filled with intensity and reverence for life. Not a fear that urges flight but that encourages us to stand up and take action.

A Model of Intelligence

From exorcism to endorcism

It's quite interesting to note that the Biblical model of spiritual intelligence is an unexpected figure, a man whose biography is full of conflict. According to the Jewish model, it would be expected that Abraham, the founder, or Moses, the prophet, would be the prime candidates. However, the role falls to Jacob. Abraham is the idealist, the self-made man, while Moses is the visionary and activist imbued with a sense of struggle; both are too absorbed in their roles and their historical moments. Because their struggles are so external to their own persons, they become archetypes and symbols. It is only when this struggle enters the realm of inner space that we find spiritual intelligence recorded in the Bible. A common (and holy) figure was needed to personify this human model.

Jacob is a model of conflict. In his immaturity, he is uncertain of his father's (Father's) love for him and insecure about his own self—an insecurity that is projected onto his brother, who occupies an envied position of legitimacy. Jacob's enemy is clear-cut, his sense of injustice goes deep, and there is an expectation of imminent disaster. He is, however, a portrait of us all, some more, some less.

It is the Biblical text itself that tells us Jacob personifies a model. This is not my own conjecture or a case of focusing on a fragment of Bible verse to back up a personal thesis, as is unfortunately so common. Jacob is given the name Israel ('he who wrestles with God'), a title granted as a spiritual initiation. This occurs in *Genesis 32:23-32*, in the middle of the story about Jacob's reunion with his brother Esau. After living in exile for twenty-one years, Jacob prepares to face an old issue with his brother. After fooling his blind father into giving him the primogeniture, Jacob was forced to flee in order to escape his brother's wrath. On the eve of their reunion, these events take place:

> *And he rose up that night [...] and passed over the ford Jabbok. [...] And Jacob was left alone; and there wrestled a Man with him until the breaking of the day. And when He saw that He prevailed not against him, He touched the hollow of his thigh; and the hollow of Jacob's thigh was out of joint, as He wrestled with him. And He said: 'Let Me go, for the day breaketh.' And he said: 'I will not let Thee go, except Thou bless me.' And He said unto him, 'What is they name?' And he said, 'Jacob.' And He said, 'Thy name shall be called no more Jacob, but Israel: for as a prince hast thou power with God and with men, and hast prevailed. And Jacob asked Him, and said: 'Tell me, I pray Thee, Thy name.' And He said, 'Wherefore is it that thou dost ask after My name?' And He blessed him there.*
>
> *And Jacob called the name of the place Peniel [face of God]: 'For I have seen God face to face, and my life is preserved.' And as he passed over Penuel the sun rose upon him, and he halted upon his thigh.*

This text not only provides us with the etymology of the word-code Israel but also gives us the context in which is arose. 'Israel' is a word that transcends the designation of a single people to become a sign that someone belongs to an order of spiritually initiated people. In other words whoever belongs to this category can be considered as '*Those who wrestle with God and with men.*'

The very setting is the place of spirituality: darkness. Nighttime opens up possibilities that light threatens. Jacob crosses a river whose name has the same letters as his (Jabbok), re-ordered, or dis-ordered, symbolic of a figure who becomes fluid and of times of transformation and change. Jacob wrestles with a man who proves to be God. Not only is the identity of this mysterious 'other' murky; the text seems to intentionally confuse aggressor and defender. Jacob and his contender switch places: first Jacob's thigh is out of joint; but at the end, it is 'Peniel' who is lame. This is inarguably a literary device to make Jacob and his antagonist one and the same person, lending the story a decidedly oneiric density, with overtones of a nightmare.

The name extracted as a blessing changes the essence of Jacob (which literally means 'he who clutches his brother's ankle') and alludes to the fact that the brothers were born twins and that Jacob came into the world grabbing onto his brother Esau's ankle. It signifies the essence of someone who is born 'being' because of a relationship with the other. Israel's center is internal, while Jacob's is external. His worldview will be characterized by senses and reverences, rather than by comparisons, analyses, or conclusions about the outer world.

Jacob comes to understand the world by externalizing what lies inside him.. He exorcises and casts out so that he can understand and master. Israel, on the other hand, brings things inside. The expression "to wrestle with God and men and to prevail over them" means integrating things and becoming internally whole. Israel will no longer see his brother as an enemy or restraint. His brother will no longer be an 'other' who is responsible for causes or consequences. He has become an Israel who has feelings in relation to others—feelings oft times of hate—but who fights only with himself.

One Biblical commentary (*Shem Sh'muel*) uses a curious method to make a revealing observation. Hebrew letters can be converted into numbers—something like the letter 'A' having the value of 1, 'B' having the value of 2, and so on. Used by Biblical commentators, this method was designated '*gematria*' or, as it is more popularly known, numerology. As we will see, its purpose is to achieve before the eyes and the mind something similar to what is accomplished by parables, those small tales that induce us to arrive at a certain conclusion or affirmation as if by experience. Their power is much greater than simply demonstrating the logic of a statement. Whoever hears the story lives it. If you look at these numbers, you will also enter a magical world of intentional or non-intentional codes that underscore and disclose certain questions.

The commentary referred to above analyzes the numerical value of the words Jacob and Israel, two words that represent not just a change in a name but in Jacob's very essence. What happened numerically between Jacob and Israel? The sum of the letters in Jacob works out to 182 while the numerical value of Israel is 541. The difference between Israel and Jacob is an increase of 359—precisely the numerical value of the word 'Satan' (which means *hindrance* or *roadblock* or, in the mythical sense, *the demon*).

The main idea behind the notion of spiritual intelligence is not that feelings or impulses should be cast out but—to the contrary—that they should be incorporated. When Jacob wrestles with his demons and makes them part of an inner struggle, without needing to demonize his brother, anyone else, or any given situation; when he assumes full responsibility for the reality around him, blaming no one; and when he places his senses and reverences in front of his fears and insecurities, then his name is Israel.

The ability to live with contradictions and paradoxes is internal. We always see the outer world as a world of efficiency in terms of measurements, decisions, and comparisons—a world that must be 'of light' because it cannot bear the mystery of darkness. But through our inner experience, we know contradiction all the time. Love that contains within itself hatred, imperfection that contains perfection, and the end that is not final—these are some of the possibilities inherent to our inner world but that do not exist in our perception of the outer world.

Spirituality does not thrive on exorcisms, as many religious traditions suggest. Perhaps this is the one non-intelligent feature that all or the great majority of religious traditions eventually develop. We can tell how far such doctrines lie from intelligent aspects of spirituality when we see how hard it is for them to live with shadows and how they need theologies that cast away unbearable darkness reveling symptoms of excessive control.

Rituals of exorcism should do just the opposite; they should not represent regurgitation but the digestion of our most contemptible features. Yet it is easy to point out that when a person incorporates his 'Satan', he changes into the devil himself. By definition, a spiritualized being is someone who travels through the 'valley of the shadow of death, but fears no evil.' This being is therefore someone who is comfortable in the darkness and who mistrusts light and clarity as tricks that reduce paradoxes to mere mistakes or incoherence. And so this person exorcises not only traditions of control and manipulation—non-intelligent forms of spirituality—but also traditions grounded solely in reason.

Sense of Goodness

The road to intolerance

> *The story goes that two friends in a restaurant ordered the same dish. When the waiter brought their plates, one steak was much bigger than the other. The friends politely started to argue that the other should choose first.*
>
> *Finally, one of them took the initiative and picked the bigger steak. Shocked, his friend couldn't help exclaiming: 'I can't believe what you just did!' The other one asked in surprise: 'What did I do?'*
>
> *'What did you do?! You saw the steaks weren't the same size, one was bigger...and that's precisely the one you took!'*
>
> *'Well, what would you have done in my place?' the first one asked. Well, of course, I would've taken the smaller one.'*
>
> *The first then responded: 'So...what's your problem?'*

The discomfort of the man who ended up with the smaller steak reveals hypocrisy. He would have felt comfortable making a sacrifice had he also been rewarded by the feeling he was being gracious. Because he was deprived the chance of being a 'good person—since his friend chose first and ignored the opportunity to be 'good' to him—getting stuck with the smaller portion was intolerable.

We accomplish part of our task of digesting and assimilating our Satan (endorcism) when we abandon this desire to 'be good'. The tension of knowing whether something is good for me or for someone else cannot be resolved in the external world, which is a world of light and control where external values and morality reign or, better put, where they tyrannize. In other words, when we try to 'be good', we are running away from dark places and trying to find keys where they weren't lost, simply because we want to look in safer, more well-lit spots.

A 'goody-goody' is a dominator who knows how to paralyze and corral someone else into the position of having to play goody-goody. The smaller steak is the price paid for binding someone else to a commitment of 'goodness', and this in itself is an act of control and domination.

One of the pillars of Western ethics and humanism is the Biblical phrase 'love thy neighbor as thyself.' Central to the ethics of Jewish monotheism and the cornerstone of Christianity (stressed by both Jesus and Rabbi Akiva, and translated into popular language by Hillel in the form of 'don't do anything to anyone else that you wouldn't want them to do to you') these words are the origin of law and of citizenship rights as we know them in the West.

One aspect of this saying, however, seems especially important to me. In its original Hebrew form, we can read instead of the word 'neighbours' (le-reecha) the word 'bad' (le-raecha) since both have the same root. The sentence would then read: 'Love your badness as you love yourself.'

Learning to love our 'bad' parts as parts of ourselves is not an apology to complacency, resignation, or imperfection. It is an act of endorcism and integration, without which tolerance cannot exist. When we realize that the word 'other' ('neighbor') has the same root as the word 'bad,' we understand a little of our own psyche. Whatever is different we automatically view as bad. Truly loving our neighbor is as difficult and violent as if we were proposing to love what is bad or imperfect. The act of exorcism, which intends to exclude and do away with what is bad, is really about trying to do away with the other, with our neighbor. How can we tolerate and love others if we don't tolerate the other inside ourselves, the part of us that does not fit norms or expectations?

There can be no identity without the other, no good without bad, and no goodness without evil. We find ourselves once again in the spiritual world of darkness, a world of tension and paradoxes. In any attempt to extirpate the 'other-bad', we run the risk of creating a monstrous 'good' that is unpleasant, horrific, and destructive. This is because love is the emotion capable of appreciating that which is different. We can only assimilate the bad that lies within us as part of ourselves if we can process it through the emotion of love.

We can only be 'good' if we undertake the spiritual work of absorbing our Satan—our own 'bad' or our own 'other'. And we are never good for our neighbor but for ourselves and for everyone. This is the only way goodness will not be a tool of domination.

> *There is a parable about a singer—the best in the land—who was brought before the king to entertain him. When the performance was over, the king was asked if he'd liked it. He said no, and offered this explanation: 'I didn't like it because he was singing for me. If he had sung for God, it would have served for me as well.'*

Goodness cannot be for our neighbor, the 'other'; it must be for everything and everyone, and then it will also serve for the other. True spiritual intelligence fears the ploys of 'goodness' with the same terror and concern that spiritual ignorance fears evil. Exorcising our 'goodness' is part of a process whereby we create room to assimilate our 'badness'.

Sense of Self-worth

We're better and worse than we imagine

> It is said that a professor of great renown was once invited to give a lecture at an affluent community in another town. The community leaders inquired how much he would charge. The professor said there was no fee and that speaking engagements were part of his duties and his mission.
>
> The lecture was scheduled and a huge crowd showed up. When the community president arrived to pick the professor up at his hotel, he was stupefied to learn over the intercom that the professor would not come down and would not fulfill his speaking engagement unless he first received twenty thousand dollars. The president argued that this demand hadn't been made earlier and that had it been, the community might never have agreed. The professor didn't care; he simply insisted that without the money there would be no lecture. It was up to them.
>
> Upset and indignant, the president consulted with key members of the community. Under pressure and disgruntled, they ended up passing a hat and gathering the amount demanded. Although they felt they'd been the victims of extortion, they gave the professor the money and he delivered his talk.
>
> The lecture was no less than spectacular. The audience was impressed by both the content of the talk and the professor's charisma. At the end, the professor went over to the community leaders and gave

them back their money. Surprised, they demanded an explanation. The man said: 'Of course I was not going to charge for the lecture, but if I didn't have the twenty thousand dollars in my pocket, I wouldn't have had the drive and enthusiasm I did.'

This story contains an interesting element of integration. Without losing sight of his internal values, the professor uses an external value—in the form of a sizeable fee—as a tool. The quality of his lecture depended in part on the money in his pocket, and the fact that he recognized this shows he was able to tolerate his own impulses without becoming a slave to them.

Spirituality is oft times portrayed as a way of putting the brakes on our impulses. This is a big mistake. As we saw earlier, spiritual intelligence only exists when there is presence, a prerequisite of any intelligence. And we cannot be present without our impulses. It is true that these same impulses breed the seven spiritual errors that Christianity has designated the 'deadly sins.' Nevertheless, these impulses are the essence of life, and they cannot be cast out but must be experienced.

An old Hasidic tale tells that the rabbis managed to lock up the 'evil impulse'. They were euphoric to find they could remove 'shadow' and 'the source of evil' from circulation. All to discover that workers quit working when they felt no ambition; that men and women quit showing interest in each other when they lost their sexual desire; and that even chickens quit laying eggs.

Our notion of holiness quite often reflects a repression of our very humanity. This notion proposes the existence of a good human being who is created by eliminating his impulses. But such a being is not human, and much less is he intelligent.

As Hasidism has defined it so well, our obligation is not to be more than we are but to be everything we are. We don't need to be saints in our quest for peace and happiness; but we need to be all we are potentially able to be. Holiness—being more—is about the realm of morality and goodness; being everything, on the other hand, places us in the realm of transgression and integration.

A man once went to speak with Rabbi Yitschak Yaakov, the Seer of Lublin, to beg the learned man to help free him from the strange thoughts that disturbed his prayers and meditation, like intruders.

No matter how hard the fellow tried to have only pure and holy thoughts, he was invaded by thoughts of envy, greed, hunger, and sex that distracted him.

'Wise man, where do these thoughts come from? Who is putting them in my head? What wicked force is trying to disturb my prayers and fool my heart?'

The sage took the man by his shoulders and urged him to calm himself.

'I don't believe these are 'strange thoughts'. Perhaps there are a few holy souls to whom thoughts like yours are strange. But your thoughts are no more than your thoughts; they are no different from mine and nothing special. On whom do you wish to blame these thoughts?'

We usually think that we can control our thoughts as if they were subject to our judgment of what is right or wrong, holy or mundane. But our worldly thoughts come and go in a way that we have no power over them. So holiness has nothing to do with 'exorcizing' these thoughts or presenting them as an intervention from external demoniacal forces. It is about dealing and working on our impulses and taking responsibility for who we are in our acts as well as in our thoughts.

It is not unusual for us to think that if we could exorcise certain thoughts, we would immediately be filled with holiness and divine grace. We often behave like the man in the story, blaming our suffering and failures on our desires. But this is not how things really are. Desire is nothing more than an emotion, just like other emotions we consider 'pure', such as love and compassion. And since desire is an emotion, it cannot be controlled. Emotions cannot be erased and much less should they be viewed as 'strange'. Of course, we don't need to make our emotions the sole determinants of our behavior. We should endeavor to make our values the determinants of our behavior.

What the story demonstrates is the wise man's warning that we can't control our emotions but rather our conduct. There is no way of thinking that is 'strange'. If you thought it, it's yours. Something caused the thought, and admitting this is a sign of maturity. The thought has something to reveal to us but it doesn't necessarily dictate what we should do. Between thought and action lies decision and free will.

The wise man's final question —'On whom do you wish to blame these thoughts?'— lays bare the disciple's spiritual immaturity. Every attempt to blame someone else is an attempt to wash our hands of responsibility. However, holiness only exists where there is involvement— that is, where there is error and recognition of error, desire and the values that manage it, risk and exposure, and, above all, contact with the human being inside of us. This is the great envy of the angels of ancient myth: although these angels recognized holiness and dwelled in its midst, unlike human beings they could not be holy. To be holy, it is essential to embrace these 'strange thoughts' as the raw material of our selves.

If we are to evaluate ourselves and have an accurate perception of our self-worth in the spiritual dimension, a tension must be present. Our impulses and fallibility are a blessing in that they are resources we can use in growing and refining our selves. For the rabbis, addressing the question of self-worth from the perspective of paradox and defining it from the realm of darkness was an inevitable exercise.

All of us should walk around with two little notes, one in each pocket, the left and the right. A Bible verse should be written on each. One should read: 'For me the world was created!' and the other: 'I am dust and to dust shall I return.' In other words, we are more and less than we imagine. If we know enough to reach into the correct pocket at the right time, we can marvel at the surprise of discovering we are better than we thought or the surprise of discovering we are worse than we thought.

Whatever form it takes, this kind of contact with reality reinforces our presence and makes us more spiritually intelligent.

Sense of Illusion

The ego as manager, never as boss

In the field of physics, any change in a medium occasions other changes, in velocity, weight, or even time. By calculating the refraction of light in water, we can determine its true path. Any understanding that does not take these different densities into account will lead to mistakes and illusions.

This is also true in the emotional, intellectual, and spiritual worlds. Today we know how to decipher the emotional world and expose our desire to see only what we want and hide what we don't want to see. These emotional interests change reality, and the role of a good therapist is to bring his client in closer touch with this reality by helping him recognize the 'media' that have impelled him to live and understand himself in a certain way.

At the same time, growing attention has been focused on the existence of hidden interests within the intellectual realm. When someone has a political commitment to understanding the world through a certain prism, this will cause refraction of his or her intellectual thinking. So-called wishful thinking reflects a kind of emotional interference on intellectuality. What is new about all this is not just that something called emotional intelligence exists but that it is a two-way street. More than distorting nature, the early twentieth-century European scientists who forced nature to fit into their racial views were demonstrating their inability to remain impartial. Like poorly calibrated lab instruments,

69

these observers subscribed to non-recognized biases that turned their results and conclusions into crude deviations from reality.

In the realm of spirituality, refractions and deviations occur when things leave and enter the medium of our individuality. If a tension, or paradox, exists inside us, it is the fact that we are differentiated while at the same time we are part of everything. We live our lives as individuals and we die as individuals. We perceive our history, our decisions, and our destinies as individual. But we know it's not quite like that. We are part of a bigger plan we cannot grasp. The words of the biologist Samuel Butler awaken us to this reality: 'The chicken is only the way an egg reproduces another egg.' In its arrogance, our individuality keeps us from realizing that we are pieces of bigger interests, of types of greater intelligence, which use us to carry out their strategies. Be that as it may, if we want to achieve peace and happiness, we must address two poles of tension: we must be the individuals that we are and, concomitantly, we must comply with the collective strategies of life as a whole.

In order to accomplish this task, we created the famous 'ego'.

Pseudo-spiritual proposals love to identify the abandonment of the ego as the center of spiritual practice. The ego is cast as an enemy to be defeated, as if it were the cause of illusion in our lives. Rabbi Zalman Schechter Shalomi always says that if someone proposes to do away with your ego, put your hand in your pocket as fast as you can and grab on to your wallet.

Inarguably, the ego can't be the top authority of our being. Reb Zalman warns us that the ego is a great manager but a lousy boss. We should not assign our final and most important decisions to it. And what does it manage? It manages customs clearance between the inside and the outside, between our inner and outer worlds. It doesn't have a small role to play and none of us is ready to leave these customs posts unattended. If we did, the outer world would feel compelled to invade us and start smuggling, at a high cost to us. However, the ego should receive new instructions from time to time that change protectionist laws and customs guarantees. Much as these decisions may often times annoy the ego and run counter to its desires, it's not up to the ego to challenge them. It's up to the boss, to our higher selves, to perceive the vital changes that become imperative to every living thing now and again. And it is also the boss's duty to undertake the arduous and oft times formidable task of training the ego-manager to follow the new rules.

Training the ego is a complicated job because the ego doesn't have exactly the same characteristics as an employee. It has a very strong tendency to inflate itself and to appropriate decision-making duties onto itself. As a key member of our team—to whom we are grateful and in whom we trust but on whom we must keep a most watchful eye—the ego is rebellious in its inflexibility.

It's easy, however, to unmask the ego whenever it usurps duties not assigned to it. The test is always 'presence'. For us to be present, we must be somewhere other than in our ego. True presence only exists in the tension between the fact that we are individuals and the fact that we are everything that is not individual. When we think in terms of our physical selves, we visualize 'everything' as represented by the heart and individuality, by the head. It is no accident that many spiritual practices try to deflate the ego through prostration. Not merely a gesture of reverence, prostration creates an important physical relation. If you bow down, you will find that your heart is higher than your head, and this is a different hierarchical representation of our selves. The being inside us that is part of everything takes priority, undermining individuality's usual position of privilege. Sometimes putting our hearts above our heads is indispensable if we are to re-establish balance in the tension between individual and everything.

Illusion always occurs when this tension between inside and outside disappears. Maintaining this tension means seeing naked reality. We need to ground ourselves in the essence and not the garments it comes clothed in. Like us, reality is a constant tension between existence and non-existence. But, as Rabbi Shefa Gold has commented, once we have known a person undressed, we no longer judge him according to his clothes.

We often realize this is one of the most important issues in training and developing our spiritual intelligence: we must be able to see this tension and perceive it as the reality that gradually frees us from deviations, refraction, and illusion.

Here is a Buddhist story:

A master and his disciple once took a trip. When they reached the bank of a river to cross, out of the corners of their eyes they both saw a frightened woman who was having trouble fording the water. According to their religion, monks are forbidden to have any type of interaction with women. The disciple immediately looked the other way and set off across the river alone.

When the disciple got to the other side, he couldn't believe his eyes. His master had picked the woman up in his arms, crossed the river, and put her down on the other side. The disciple said nothing and they continued on their way.

Some time later, still upset by what had happened at the river, the disciple mustered the courage to ask: 'Master, we know we are not supposed to even look at a woman, much less carry one. How do you account for your behavior?'

The master stared deep into his disciple's eyes and said: 'Woman? I carried a woman from one bank to another. But you...you're still carrying her.'

Rules, norms, and structure are what nourish the ego. Like a bird's nest built of twigs or any other available material, the ego builds itself out of whatever it captures from reality. The amalgam of the ego is comprised of bits and pieces of what people say about us, their criticisms, fragments of our past experiences, and all sorts of expressions of affection or rejection. The master in this story shows his disciple a larger being, one who makes decisions without needing to cling so fiercely to norms order to survive. The ego feels threatened when rules are broken and, as we have seen, its skills are purely managerial in nature. The ego vetoes, or at least cautions against, anything that goes outside the box, that entails creativity and risk.

It is the disciple, however, who really jeopardizes the spirit of the law and the essence of things. As he prioritizes self-preservation, reality is refracted--what we call an illusion. Though the disciple believes he is right, it is because of his rigid structure of rights and wrongs that he ends up being wrong. The master's job is to free him from this illusion and make him see correctly.

Whenever we find ourselves facing risks or chasms in our lives, we seek refuge in our egos, for they are known turf. Just as people are told to protect themselves during an earthquake by standing in a doorway, the ego—customs official between our inner and outer worlds—acts as a similar protective mechanism during catastrophes. This is its job, and that's why we are so protective and careful about our egos: we depend upon them to lend us a feeling of security. But this is quite clearly a fleeting security. If you find yourself in an earthquake, you're much better off getting out of the house as quickly as possible rather than standing in a doorway. Staying inside means closing yourself up in a dangerous place that might not withstand the tremors but may collapse instead. The greatest self is the one that manages to leave the house and look at it from the outside. If it collapses, it will not take the essence along with it.

Something else that causes the ego to produce bits of illusion is its constant bad habit of acting out parts. The ego's lack of 'presence' turns it into a phantom that can only find life by inventing a drama where it can play a role. Unmasking the ego means revealing its 'non-presence', that is, how it is only a character and *not* the author or creator.

> *The story goes that in a certain region of Europe, it hadn't rained for months. The farmers were desperate. Following Jewish tradition in such situations, a day was marked for fasting and praying. From Biblical times, fasting has been associated with repentance and concentration, ingredients deemed vital to petitional prayer and rituals.*
>
> *So the city scheduled a day of prayer and fasting to ask for rain. Everyone congregated at the synagogue, but the rabbi didn't show up.*
>
> *The town folk decided to check his house and, much to their surprise, they found him there enjoying lunch.*
>
> *They asked: 'Excuse us for disturbing you, most honored rabbi, but perhaps you don't know today was declared a day of fasting?'*
>
> *Demonstrating no emotion, the rabbi responded ironically: 'Fast? Why?'*
>
> *Because, rabbi, we're facing a very serious drought. That's why we've gathered at the synagogue and have great faith that a miracle will happen.'*
>
> *The rabbi then went to his window and, watching the crowd hurrying towards the synagogue, said: 'Faith? They're all going to pray for rain but I don't see a single one of them carrying an umbrella.'*

This is 'non-presence': they believe but they don't believe. They play act at believing but they are not fully present in what they do. Spirituality is represented by a tree—the Tree of Life—precisely because it has not only a set of branches that turn upwards, toward the heavens, but a set of 'branches', or roots, that turn downwards, into the ground. Without ground, without a good understanding of the illusions surrounding us, we lack the ballast needed for us to stretch our arms up to the heavens. First and foremost, spirituality is the art of having roots.

Sense of Serving

The issue isn't so much being loved as loving

If the ego isn't the boss, then who is?

For many, at least in terms of spirituality, the answer should point to the Creator as the most qualified candidate for the position. However, spiritual intelligence does not embrace the idea of an all-responsible God but of a God who shares responsibility. It is this act of partnership, this being together in suffering and in pleasure, that creates the notion of compassion (to hold the other's *passio*, i.e., their pain). A God-boss would not be compassionate nor would His creatures be good to Him. Crowning and praising God can easily be transformed from an act of devotion into a desire to put the blame on whoever is the boss in charge of things and of reality itself. We're all attracted to the idea that there is a level of power and order that lets us declare: 'Call the manager. I'll only talk to the supervisor. I want to complain!' This is why many people pay tithes to their temples, religions, or traditions—so they can make demands and lodge complaints. The more God is responsible for everything that happens to us, the more we can complain and blame Him. But the position of boss is not outside us nor is it up above.

Once again, in order to understand who the 'boss' is, we must integrate contradictions. On the one hand lies our individuality—we are our own bosses—and on the other, we are tied to projects larger than our own identity: we serve some purpose. Whenever we realize that we are serving, we leave behind the slavery and managerial mediocrity of our egos and report directly to the boss.

We can better understand the concept of serving if we ask ourselves 'to whom or what do I serve?' or 'to whom or what do I *not* serve?' These questions often gain existential and sometimes philosophical, ideological, or theological pretense. In any case, our peace and happiness depend upon the answers, and these answers most decidedly are not gratuitous or superfluous matters.

The very concept of spirituality intermingles with the idea of 'serving'. Any notion of transcendence—that is, any notion that we are not contained solely in our individuality or our existence—falls into the realm of spirituality. Verbs like 'fulfill' or 'serve' are essential to human well-being. Without going into the matter of 'fulfilling what' or 'fulfilling for whom', it's worth remembering that these verbs apply to all of spirituality, not only spirituality grounded in religion. All human effort to master one of these verbs reflects a form of spirituality. 'Fulfill and serve' are words that can be found in the vocabularies of causes, ideologies, dreams, missions, systems of organization, laws, and commitments, in addition, of course, to religious beliefs and traditions.

The act of serving expresses an intimate relationship with life—a form of refinement. When we serve in the spiritual sense, we serve everyone. In traditional language, whoever serves God, serves everyone. When we serve false gods, we do not serve everyone. We serve only ourselves or a specific group.

We are constantly given opportunities to serve but most of the time we aren't paying attention. There's a phrase in the Bible that evokes the issue of serving. When God looks for Adam and Eve in paradise, just after they have eaten the forbidden fruit, he asks: *aiEKHa?* (Where are you?). This question is almost a compass for the spiritual world. 'Where are you?' is a question that should be answered with the following statement: *Hineni* (Here I am). But we can't answer this way unless we are truly present, ready to serve.

It's interesting to note that another question formed of the same root as '*aiEKHa?*' is the expression '*EiKHa?*' (*How can that be?*) to be found at the opening of the book of Lamentations. The letters that denote presence and encounter are the same ones that signify being lost, adrift. One question affirms the meaning of life while the other questions it. This is something we are familiar with not only in the collective realm—where a steady resistance to serving can result in perverse and violent relationships—but also at the level of individual experience. Depression moves in and life loses meaning when someone cannot truthfully respond to the question 'Where are you?' If we fail to respond time after time, the summons and the chance to serve are transformed into the despair expressed in the question: 'How come?'.

Perhaps we should take another look at the question 'Who's the boss?'

The following story is told about the legendary Hanina Ben Dosa, a second-century rabbi who was considered a fair and simple person. His ability to serve gained him great renown, for his prayers were always heard and answered.

> *Once when the son of Yohanan Ben Zakai—the most important rabbi of his generation—fell ill, Rabbi Yohanan sought the help of Rabbi Hanina. Hanina put the young man's head in his lap and prayed for his recovery. His plea was answered. Rabbi Yohanan then said: 'If I had prayed, I wouldn't have been successful!'*
>
> *His wife was offended. 'What?' she exclaimed. 'What makes him any more deserving than you?'*
>
> *Rabbi Yohanan then clarified: 'The difference between us is one of roles not of merit. Rabbi Hanina is, in a manner of speaking, a servant of God's, while I am his minister. A minister needs to schedule an appointment but a servant comes and goes as he pleases.'*

It is a very singular relationship with life that gives someone access to all the 'dressing rooms' and other spaces that lie behind tightly closed doors, places where even great masters and authorities have problems getting in without special passes. The sages, the doctors, the leaders, and other figures of authorities stand in these lines. But those who serve coffee come and go as they please. Serving is the most powerful key card in this existence.

This is the secret of someone who serves: he or she is headed in the opposite direction of the ego. While the ego makes its greatest goal to be loved, whoever serves chooses the act of loving. The most important thing for someone who serves is the pleasure of being able to love. This pleasure in itself suffices, and in most cases it causes the person who loves to be loved by others as well.

Management of our lives may lie in the hands of our facet that wants to be loved, but it will only be efficient if it respects the guidelines and strategies handed down by the part of us that loves and serves. As confusing and paradoxical as it might seem, serving is not an act of submission or subordination. On the contrary, it is the most magnanimous, independent behavior we can adopt. While someone who seeks to be loved is always tied to and dependent upon the other, the one who loves is a free and independent being. The ego does not serve but is servile, because it draws its sustenance from the external world; but the boss who loves and serves draws its sustenance from the inner world.

Rabbi Yohanan is the ego whereas Rabbi Hanina is the servant. The former represents authority and external recognition; the latter represents inner singularity and naturalness. One is the minister, the other is the servant; one is important, the other is efficacious. One performs and directs; the other takes risks and reaps the greatest yield.

One of the most meaningful proofs of spiritual intelligence is how much emphasis we place on the power of loving to the detriment of 'being loved'. The more we serve, instead of being served, the greater the intelligence. The ultimate model of this intelligence—the Creator—is described in the following words by the Rabbi of Karlin: 'May I love someone who is wonderful in the same way the Creator loves a wicked man!'

Loving is not an act of altruism but the most complete form of well-being. Someone who loves is not a holy or pious person, as religion has asserted. Loving represents a balance between disinterest and egoism. It is the way we express ourselves wholly and integrally.

Sense of Offering

Fear, mistrust, and confusion on the altar

We have examined the notion that the more we serve or the more we love, or the less we are served or the less we depend upon being loved, the greater our spiritual intelligence. The greater our independence—so that we can enjoy life without waiting for others to prove their love or without compiling dossiers on how others are unfair or how they are to blame for our misfortunes—the greater this intelligence.

If we want to take the path to developing this intelligence, we must be able to make offerings. As much as it may seem archaic and ritualistic, this concept is fundamental in the spiritual world. Making an offering does not mean giving gifts in order to bribe the world up above but it does mean knowing how to sacrifice certain aspects of our being which keep us from growing and changing. Like animals that shed their skins every so often, or like the butterfly that casts off weighty parts of its body in order to fly, we human beings must also undergo a kind of self-recycling.

These abandoned 'cocoons' that allow us to take spiritual flight have to do with three of the dimensions mentioned earlier: physical, emotional, and intellectual. When we offer up these 'burdens' and burn them on the altar of life, we are initiating ourselves into a new level of spiritual intelligence. Let us identify these burdens or obstacles by: in the physical dimension, they are our fears; in the emotional dimension, our mistrust; and in the intellectual dimension, our confusion.

Let's look at each of them separately.

Our physical world teaches us to fear. This fear is a survival tool that helps guide us in making a vital decision: whether to fight or to flee. But as time goes by and we accumulate greater life experience, residual fears built up and eventually constitute a roadblock within our spiritual world. The Rabbi of Ger said: 'Fear should only be a feeling of reverence for God. Nothing else should be feared. When we realize we are feeling afraid, we should know this is a misguided emotion, deviated away from the only source deserving of fear. All fear is a form of idolatry, for to fear is to revere that which is feared; it is to make an offering to that which is feared.'

We don't realize that our fears are an offering to our gods, and 'god' with a small 'g' represents spiritual ignorance. This 'god' means imprisonment to conditioning and to internal orders that tell us what we should do and what we shouldn't do. God (with a capital 'G') means 'duties' and 'prohibitions' but not ones compelled by ordinary fear. The fear of God constitutes both a form of reverence as well as such a deep connection with life that in itself, spontaneously, it presupposes duties and proscriptions. However, the human being is present and involved in this process, which is born from the wrestling 'with this God.' Gods with a small 'g'—whether it is the god of the volcano, or the god that helps us past tests, or 'my god'—all represent the ordinary fears we offer up as idolaters (i.e., as the spiritually ignorant). We want to appease these gods and win their favor in order to quell our fears. And just as these gods are controllable, so do they control us.

Spiritual intelligence depends upon reverence, but distinguishing it from fear is a hard task. Fear does not permit reverence but instead replaces it, transforming 'senses' and perceptions into superstition and false beliefs?

We need to realize that the source of our fears is our body, our physical world. The fear of falling, the fear of hurting ourselves, the fear of seeing what we don't want to, the fear of hearing what we don't want to, the fear of having to pay the price. Every unpleasant experience in life, every experience that involves physical suffering, or every uncertainty that often times allows this suffering to happen, transforms itself into fear. And this fear then turns into an empty shell and a burden. Burning this discarded shell on the altar and replacing it with reverence is more than a symbolic act. It is to cut ourselves free from ties that won't let us fly or transform ourselves.

Every offering involves turning over something we want to change. The fire of this sacrifice is an honest, courageous look at reality that will transform fear into reverence. And something that was only material, something of no use to the spiritual world, becomes something acceptable and useful. Not just a kind of donation, an offering is about our ability to offer up something useful to the dimension of the spirit. Sometimes we don't know how to give someone a present because we fail to understand the recipient's true needs. This offering is about learning to understand these needs. And like every encounter or every form of intelligence, the pleasure of giving is just as great as the pleasure of receiving.

On the emotional level, the equivalent of fear is mistrust. Built out of the lingering disappointments, frustrations, and lack of support experienced throughout our lives, it is mistrust the very essence of what is offered at the altar. Whenever the maternal breast fails to arrive in time or does not satiate us, the result is worse than absence itself. It engenders distrust. The raw material of this mistrust is our inability to separate what we know from what we don't know. The unknown is a deep abyss and if we stare into it too long, vertigo will throw us off balance, even if we have both feet planted firmly on the ground. Like the story of the yogi who liked to stand on his head next to a chasm. When asked how he found the courage to do it, he said he just imagined he was doing it in his own room.

There is no difference between the abyss and our own room when we have confidence and trust, and that is our reality. Perhaps we'd like to argue that the room presents no danger but then we are turning away from reality and favoring the unknown and the risky in detriment of the known. If we can separate the known-safe from the unknown-uncertain, we create firm ground where we can stand on our heads, even if beside an abyss. However, only you yourself can perceive that the firm and safe is just as (or more) real than what is uncertain.

Choosing the 'full half glass' does not depend solely on our memories of things past but also on how we deal with obstacles. It takes intelligence—in other words, it is a display of efficacity—to choose to imagine the room rather than think about the abyss. If you see a room instead of an abyss, you'll stand on your head many more times in your life. A mistrustful person would say: 'But the abyss only needs to become real one single time and it voids the efficacy of all these headstands.' This is the fear produced by gods with a small 'g'. But the intelligence of senses and reverences makes us see that the notion of 'room' is about acting instead of reacting, about living instead of simply surviving. Choosing trust, with its risks and its costs, expands life, while mistrust narrows it. *Trust is a type of emotional courage.* Just as fear should not be experienced as something outside but inside us and should be transformed into reverence, mistrust should be experienced internally, as a form of faith.

The secret to achieving this trust lies in making offerings. Whenever we feel mistrustful, we should shun close proximity with people filled with trust, and we should likewise not force ourselves to stand too close to an abyss. We must remember that trust is not an external conquest and if we behave as if it were, we will quite likely augment our mistrust. Each person at his own pace must take the product of his efforts, of his slow and gradual ability to rid himself of his mistrust, and serve these up as offerings.

The same thing happens with intellectual fear, which is expressed in our confusion or in an understanding that contains idolatry. There is a Hasidic parable that can help us better comprehend this concept. The parable compares the figures of the philosopher and the prophet, as representatives of the intellectual world.

> *Two men were invited to the king's palace. The wiser of the two went straight up to the king's throne. The less wise, however, was so impressed by the riches and beauty of the palace that he forgot why he had come there: to speak to the king.*

Confusion is a product of this curious eye bedazzled by reality's complexity and details. Not that there is anything wrong or vulgar about noticing the grandeur of beautiful, refined things – much to the contrary. This is the very function of the intellect --- to allow us to comprehend sophistication, which also produces reverence. The minor philosopher, however, forgets about the senses that tie him to his true reverence. The greater philosopher—the prophet—does not live by the superficial features of reason or the adornments of reality alone. He knows there are principles that built the palace, principles much more magnificent and enlightening than external analysis. The wisest thing to do is rush to the room where you will find the Intelligence that makes palaces.

As mentioned earlier, certainty applied to doubt yields the intellect's most sophisticated product. Even so, this process brings with it confusion and for this reason will serve false gods. It is doubt applied to doubt itself, as likewise mentioned earlier, that frees the philosopher and makes him a prophet or visionary.

> *Someone told the Rabbi Pinchas of Korets that a wise man by the name of Spinoza had once declared that the human being has the same nature as animals and that in no way is he above the creatures.*
>
> *The rabbi smiled and said: 'Someone should ask this freethinker if the animals can produce among themselves a thinker like Spinoza.*

The rabbi in the story shines doubt on the certainty of the thinker's doubt. It's not that we shouldn't see sovereign and independent intellectual production as a form of intelligence. It's just that if a philosopher wants to be truly profound and not merely a maze of thoughts, from time to time he must offer up his accumulated confusions. Burning confusion on the altar is not a betrayal of the quality of thought but will connect it with the ultimate reason for being in the palace.

By offering up our fear, mistrust, and confusion, we produce in ourselves a carefree courage to live—something we know as happiness.

Sense of Revelation

Looking for truth instead of certainty

One of the least understood themes in relation to spiritual intelligence has to do with revelations. Most spiritual traditions have built themselves around a presumed revelation. But if revelation belongs to the spiritual world, how can we say this is a dimension where doubts apply to doubts? If something is revealed, then shouldn't we be speaking of certainties—as today's fundamentalist streams of thought contend? After all, if a prophet is a vehicle for bringing divine guidance to our sphere, shouldn't we consider the spiritual universe to be the ultimate realm of certainty?

What happens is that when these revelations are produced by a spiritual intelligence, they are never certainties but only truths. And truths admit the existence of other, opposite truths. Certainty, on the other hand, is dictatorial. Truths have to do with human quests whereas certainties have to do with our deep-rooted desire for control. Truths are generated through conflict and experience. In their conception, they are absolute yet flexible, like everything having to do with the most profound wisdom. This is because *knowing is not something we possess but rather an ongoing contact with life*. Truth is dynamic and malleable to life.

One of the most common mistakes we make is to search for certainties that will appease our questions and queries. If we would search for truths instead, we would discover not only that they are available to us but also that they tell us more than certainties. Yet people look for manuals, for how-to books, and they lose touch with the most vital element of truths—doubts and uncertainties.

> *There is a story about a sterile woman who went to a rabbi to ask him to bless her so that she might have the child she longed for. The rabbi said: 'I can't work a miracle, but I know a woman in a similar situation who went to a rabbi for the same reason. And the rabbi told her the same thing I'm telling you, and she left his office, came back a little while later with a prayer shawl, and gave it to the rabbi as a present. A few weeks later, she was pregnant.'*
>
> *The women left and a few hours later returned with a prayer shawl for the rabbi. 'No, my child,' the rabbi said patiently, 'the woman I told you about had never heard this story!'*

Answers related to truths cannot be copied; they are not certainties like laboratory results that can be replicated an infinite number of times. The Rabbi of Kotzk used to say: 'Everything in this world can be imitated except for truth, since a truth that is imitated is no longer a truth.' It cannot be imitated yet at the same time it is absolute. How can that be? If something is complete, unconditional—as we perceive truths to be—why can't they be imitated? Why is it that the barren woman who reproduced the same situation as the first woman failed to achieve the same results? The rabbi patiently explains to her that he is not a reference point for certainties but for truths. Blessings and surprises come as the product of an individual's ability to get in touch with the purest springs of reality, which we have come to call truths. The woman who became pregnant managed to get in touch with her desire to have a child and expressed it through a wholly spontaneous gift. From the depths of this gift, her uterus is opened. Armed with this truth sculpted out of life, comes the answer, along with the fantastic feeling that our needs have been met.

Spiritual ignorance believes that our requests are met because there's a system of lines up above, where everyone takes a number. As if faith were made up of certainties, like one more consumer good. We must remember that all spiritual reality is made up of darkness. Light and certainties make searches more pleasant but they don't lead us to 'keys'. From the angle of a certainty, it doesn't make sense to believe that a prayer shawl will cause fertility. But as a 'truth', the episode narrated by the rabbi is inarguably efficacious.

Truths and revelations constitute sacred paradoxes. Like everything else that is spiritual and owes its existence to a tension, truth is an absolute that is relative, something unlimited that is limited, and a doubt that is more fitting and responds better than a certainty.

Those who know the nature of truth suffer when they see individuals, or even an entire civilization, chasing after certainties to respond to their main questions. The answers are available but they are ignored, because we lack the spiritual apparatus needed to see them.

The following commentary by Rabbi Pinkas is enlightening. He said:

> *'It is written that he who lives his life rightly should see with eyes that do not see and hear with ears that do not hear. And this is an important teaching! Because what I see most in my daily routine as a rabbi is people coming to me for advice and bringing questions that they answer with their own questions.'*

The rabbi is surprised to find the answers lodged inside the questions themselves. Obviously these answers are not certainties but truths. And since they are truths, they can't be imitated or repeated and they don't look like what we would normally regard as a 'key'. That's why it is important to see with eyes that do not see and hear with ears that do not hear. Seeing (in order to believe) and hearing (in order to witness) are our most precise tools for measuring certainties. To discover truths, human beings must also see and hear—but with eyes trained to look without seeing and ears that listen but don't hear.

Truths are only revealed in the dimension where they do not exist as a consumer good, and therefore they cannot be transmitted. They can be shared but they cannot be taught or copied. This is what's wrong with the fellow who climbs up on his soapbox in a public square and tries to convince passersby of something. Convincing people has to do with certainties and not truths, precisely because the latter cannot be transmitted or taught. Every attempt to convince or convert someone else is an act of spiritual ignorance, one that involves a market of certainties but never of truths.

Truths are of no good over loudspeakers!

It is said that a huge multitude once crowded tightly aroud the Rabbi of Apt to hear his teachings.

'This will do you no good,' he shouted to the people. 'Those of you who are ready to hear my teachings will hear them no matter how far away; those who aren't ready to hear them won't hear them no matter how close.'

A person can only be converted if he or she is filled with certainties. This is how so-called brainwashing works. People are stuffed with certainties that fill up spaces meant for truths, thereby eliminating tensions and, in turn, doubts and uncertainties. We can say that faith is a break which occurs at a given moment in the process of questioning and searching, but it is never the beginning of this process. The 'certainty' of faith is forged in the fire of our deepest doubts. It is holy doubt that we apply to doubts, transforming them into senses which should never be confused with knowledge. Thanks to our reverences, we can discern light in the midst of darkness but this will never constitute the obviousness of clarity. These reverences may seem unmistakable to us because of their enlightened essence but they will never constitute the unequivocal of certainty.

The danger of spiritual ignorance is that it is more perverse than a lack of faith. An atheist or someone with a rational mentality is restricted to aspects of reality that can be 'proved'. Their discernment is leery of relying on senses and reverences and they reject doubts as dispensable. Someone who is spiritually ignorant, however, confuses truth forged out of profound doubt with certainties, at the intellectual level. The latter person believes that the enlightenment he or she experienced in the midst of darkness constituted clarity. And a revelation is transformed into doctrine, and we leave the sphere of interpreting reality and find ourselves in the sphere of power.

Sense of Tolerance

Answer and power

Revelation is to a question as doctrine is to an answer; the former is to truth as the latter is to certainty. We hardly ever realize it but what sheds greater light on us is not an answer but its relationship of tension with the question that produced it. Unless we have a clear perception of the questions, the answers will be cold and empty. We can synthesize these notions by saying that wisdom does not let go of the tension between a question and an answer once an answer has been found. Furthermore, spirituality is the application of 'fear, mistrust, and confusion' to the answer and not to the question. Let's see if we can understand this better.

The magic and holiness of the Biblical text, for example, are revealed in the relationship of tension between its questions and answers. Or we could put it this way: this tension has been experienced down through the centuries as the tension between revelation and doctrine. On the one hand, the text serves the purpose of revelation—in other words, its interpretive character demands exegesis and commentary. On the other, it has served as the source of doctrines and dogmas that today (perhaps more than at any other time) make up the religious map of the West.

The text itself is inarguably a revelation in that it has produced truths. How do we know this? Because the text has produced and still produces certainties that are and will no longer be certainties, as befits the nature of interpretation. The exercise of interpreting and reinterpreting keeps the text open—immutable and flexible, in a fine paradox, as spirituality requires. It is likewise inarguable that this process has generated the greatest spiritual ignorances ever known in history. And that should come as no surprise. The doubts applied to doubts by one generation become certainties, and these become codified in commentaries and conduct. These 'certainties' are handed down to the next generation, whose work is redoubled: it must take the 'truths' of the past and render them flexible again—and only then is it possible to interact with them. But if these truths remain standing as 'certainties', then doctrines will prevail and the past will become a spiritual burden for the present. If on the contrary they are perceived as the truths of the past, they will constitute a valuable legacy for the present. Thus we can stand upon the shoulders of past generations and see farther. And 'farther' does not just mean we can look for better answers but, to the contrary, we can delve more deeply into questions and anxieties as well.

The extent to which a tradition or holy text is spiritualized can be seen in how tolerant its doctrines (or the past perceived as doctrine) are towards the revelation received by new generations. The Torah (the text revealed on Mount Sinai) is revealed again to each new generation, so long as it is this generation's vocation to produce truths. In this case, the revelation will be more concerned with reopening and revitalizing questions than with reopening and revitalizing the answers produced in the past. Or, as stated earlier, when fear, mistrust, and confusion are applied not to the questions that are a product of the present (as is common) but when they focus on the answers produced in the past. Note that it is not a matter of abandoning them as dispensable but rather of incorporating them as the raw material and asset of our present doubts.

It is curious how science abhors doctrines because they hinder free thinking but, as far as spiritual matters go, both science and doctrine have a lot in common. Doctrine has to do with the sphere of knowledge (certainty applied to certainties) while science has to do with the sphere of understanding (doubts applied to certainties). Both are partners in their antagonism towards the risk and uncertainty produced by senses and reverences. While we can make an exception for the new approaches adopted in the most advanced areas of science, where the effort is to incorporate a greater degree of uncertainty and improbability into reality, it must be stated that sciences and doctrines are fruits of the desire for power and not of any unbiased interest in interpreting reality.

Fanaticism and consumerism are flip sides of the same coin, and no 'spiritual' doctrine has expressed this better than utopian socialism. In its outlook, utopian socialism contained a proposal of prophetic radicalism that exposed the ultimate interest of doctrines and sciences, i.e., to be tools of power. Utopian socialism's worldview and understanding of reality are steeped in reverences. The proposal is built upon an equality found nowhere in nature. From human beings, it expects a generosity and maturity corresponding to great faith. Instead of asking whether God exists—doubting doubts and producing faith in this belief—it applies doubts to doubts concerning human limitations and its produces faith in an ethical human being. This man, in the image and likeness of an absolute ideal, follows from a long line of prophets, including Moses, Buddha, Isaiah, Ezekiel, and Jesus. More than faith in God, all of those cited had faith in His lesser image and likeness—the human being. And because they were enlightened people who without any naiveté understood human vicissitudes and the human desire for power, they had great faith in people, much more faith than most of us are capable of.

At the root of the desire for power lies the desire for control. We need to have control in order to stave off death. This is the messianic dream of so many streams of thought that demonstrate spiritual ignorance. The expectation that reality will one day consist solely of certainties is the cruelest desire we live with. In Genesis, the Biblical text warns of this danger in the symbolism of the Tree of Knowledge, as it also does through the Tower of Babel. Human beings may understand their 'image and likeness' to refer to something external rather than internal. They can hope to be like the absolute projection of themselves externally and thus live in illusion. Or they can have so much faith in themselves that they believe in what is most improbable—a human being intelligent enough to see in the dark, to know before knowing, and to act in reverence.

Fanaticism and consumerism want to place what is outside inside, the former by means of certainty and the latter by means of ownership. If we keep this in mind, the pro-tradition and pro-property stances often taken by certain fascist groups make perfect sense. Certainty guarantees ownership, and ownership guarantees certainty. From this angle we can see that all emphasis on answers derives from a desire for power. An answer that quickly gets rid of its originating question, rather than preserving a relationship of tension with it, manifests a hidden agenda of power and control.

George Santayana said: 'Fanaticism consists in redoubling your effort when you have forgotten your aim.' Fanaticism puts the answer at the top of the agenda; in fact, it even forgets the question or would like to be rid of it on purpose. By taking another road of certainty, fanaticism wants to achieve science's hidden agenda: control. Its concepts are based not on a life process that gradually offers up for sacrifice its fears, mistrusts, and confusions but rather on banishment, suppression, and exorcism. The extreme opposite of spirituality is not materialism or science but fanaticism. As stated by the comentator *Hafetz Chaim*: 'With faith, there are no questions; without faith, there are no answers.' There is a paradox that is probably our most important tool in reading reality, as long as it maintains its tension. If the tension is lost, however, we end up with the answers without questions established by the fanatic's faith, or the questions without answers established by the scientist's lack of faith. Doubts applied to doubts produce truths that are indispensable to answers but they also produce the malevolent effect of certainties.

Unlike truths, certainties are a trick. And like all tricks, they don't really work; they just seem to. How they operate is simple, as we saw before. They absorb answers and throw away questions, destroying any evidence that might in the future call these answers into question. Every answer is a political proposal and expresses power. An answer that is good for one thousand years is just what a dictator needs. It is always his goal to destroy the seed that could breed a new answer.

An answer without its question is closed and intolerant; it is the concrete realization of a desire.

> *Intolerance is the reaction of someone who is afraid, mistrustful, or confused, and its chief role is to hide questions and essences.*
>
> *A man once went to the Rabbi of Kotzk and said he was having trouble: 'People call me a fanatic. Why do they accuse me of this disease? Why can't they see I'm a pious person?'*
>
> *The rabbi replied: 'A fanatic makes major questions into minor ones, and minor questions into major ones.'*

When we observe our lives more closely, we realize how fanatical we are. Sadness, irritation, and intolerance are fanatical acts since they generally emphasize what is irrelevant and relegate what is essential to a second level.

Tolerance is the measure of spirituality. We're not talking about complacency or condescension but about sincere tolerance that can sustain all living questions and not bury them like criminal evidence of the answer. No matter how self-assured and convinced a person might be, his or her commitment must always be to the question and never to the answer. Only the fanatic has a pact with the answer. If you are spiritualized, you never sell your soul to the answer. Convictions should source their nourishment from the tension lying between question and answer and should never fear or distrust this tension. Signs of fear and mistrust show how much confusion lies within such convictions.

If you are not ready to sacrifice your answer—your one and so dearly beloved answer—you do not share the legacy of Abraham, ready to sacrifice his 'only and beloved son/convictions.' But what looks to us like a sacrifice, a holocaust of an answer, gives birth to a truth that had always been alive behind the old answer.

The only way to free a fanatic or a spiritually ignorant person is by restoring his tolerance of himself. The device of projecting one's intolerance of oneself onto the external world is well known. By showing intolerance towards the world around him, the fanatic finds respite from his intolerance towards himself. There is no doubt that the fanatic is to spirituality what autoimmune diseases are to health. Autoimmune diseases are an intensification of the immune system that prompts an organism to attack not only unwanted micro-organisms but also the organism itself. Defense is as indispensable as it is potentially lethal. In the spiritual realm, the search for answers can make us victims of relentless attacks by these same answers.

The story goes that a fanatic went to talk to Rabbi Mordechai of Lechovitch.

'Rabbi, I'll do /* make any penitence that is asked of me. Fasts, mortification, abstinence…just advise me and I'll do them all, as long as I can pay for my sins!'

93

The rabbi replied: 'And will you do everything I instruct you to do, without questioning it or changing my recommendations, either to the left or to the right?'

'I'll do everything, I'll make good on every word!' the contrite man answered.

'Well then, pay attention. Every morning you're going to get up and make yourself a fine breakfast, with everything you like best. At lunch and at dinner, you'll treat yourself extremely well, and never forget to have a good bottle of wine with your food. Make sure you sleep in a very comfortable bed, and see to it that you always get a good night's sleep. Don't do anything you find unpleasant and whatever you do, don't punish yourself with any form of self-mortification. Come back in a year and we'll see what we'll do then.'

The penitent couldn't believe it. He had prepared himself to hear the harshest demands, and these were his instructions?

Once back to his routine, he found himself tortured by the same thoughts: 'Here I am, a sinner who is constantly rebelling against his Creator and who drags his soul from the heights to the depths of corruption—how can I delight in the pleasures of this world and indulge myself this way?' At each meal, he went through the same torture; he went around feeling crushed and could find no peace. Although he had started out a rather heavyset man, by the end of the year he was pale and gaunt. He barely had the strength to go see the rabbi when the time came.

The rabbi looked at the devastated man and said: 'Enough already!'

And he advised the man to lead a normal life, neither indulging himself so extravagantly nor punishing himself so harshly. The man lived out the rest of his days happy and serene.

As an antidote to so much intolerance, the rabbi prescribed an intolerable dose of tolerance. The rabbi used the cruelty of an intolerant man who had to be tolerant of himself as a kind of shock treatment, exposing exposed the man's disease. He found pleasure in martyrdom and self-punishment. The rabbi couldn't prescribe something as pleasurable as suffering if his intention was to help the man change. Every fanatic should be dealt with in this manner. Answers camouflage confusion; questions provide truths. Living a year in a permanent state of questioning, experiencing the profound pleasure of questions, with their liberating options and possibilities, is the detox treatment that fanatics need in order to recover the holy tension between question and answer. The choice is to tolerate or be ignorant.

Sense of Connectedness

The more we're alone, the more we're together

Our loneliness is the main reason we're drawn to answers. As soon as we are born, we experience the existence of the maternal breast that awaits us—and with it, a mother, a family, a society, and an agenda for growing and developing. But on the other hand, we face the uncertainty of whether the breast will reach our lips, whether the care and attention of our parents and our society will meet our needs, and whether our development will be interrupted by death.

All the devices life offers us to satisfy our needs cannot undo the fact that we are alone. The maternal breast might not be there, because we and our mothers are no longer a single being. The other—our neighbor—might not be there for us and we might not be there for the other, because we are separate, each of us alone. This is what strikes us so hard about the reality of death: those closest to us have their own destiny, just as we have our own destiny, independent from them. There is, however, a link, fine as a strand of hair, that binds destinies, individuals, and independent realities. On the one hand, nowadays this connection is supported by ecology—which tells us that each individual and each species intersects with everything else—while at the same time it is forsaken by individualism, which ranks quality of life above any other value. It is worth our while to ask what kind of connection this is that everyone claims to believe in, even though no one is 'going outside with an umbrella in hand'.

A friend told me she and her parents went to meet with the rabbi who was going to officiate at her *bat-mitzva* (religious confirmation). According to my friend, the rabbi kept reciting over and over, in stock phrases and catchwords: 'Everything is connected, everything is connected.' When the family left, they went home making fun of the cliché: everything is connected. Clichés are portraits of what we 'believe in' but not so much that they'll prompt us to carry an umbrella. The commonplace 'everything is connected' contains a notion that we need to recoup and transform into a sense.

The first step to recovering this sense of connectedness is learning to endure being alone. This is usually hard for us to do because we confuse being alone with loneliness and isolation. We struggle desperately to make everything connected but on the outside, externally. If we can own and accumulate things, then we feel connected. The feeling that we have a home, a family, a dog, a car, and so on lets us experience a false sense of connectedness. Another very common trick is to try to live someone else's life in order to reduce our own loneliness. This trick that seems to connect us—sometimes leaving us inseparable from and dependent on the other—is an illusion that leads to dissatisfaction and frustration.

> *The story goes that a businessman went to talk to a rabbi. The man complained that he had opened a shop on the same street as a competitor and the competitor was getting much more business than he was. The man wanted the rabbi to tell him why he was falling behind the competition.*
>
> *The rabbi said: 'Maybe he has better-quality or cheaper goods.' To which the businessman replied: 'I've seen everything he has and I've got the same things, but cheaper.'*
>
> *'Maybe he has a better choice of articles,' suggested the rabbi.*
>
> *'Impossible. I keep up on everything he has and in addition to what he sells, I sell a lot of things he doesn't.'*
>
> *'Perhaps its the number of sales clerks?'*
>
> *'I know how many he has and I've hired more than him.'*
>
> *'Maybe his store hours are more convenient?'*
>
> *'Impossible. I know his hours and I open earlier and close later.'*
>
> *And then the rabbi declared: 'I know what your trouble is!'*
>
> *'What?' the businessman asked, both curious and defensive.*

'You're so busy keeping an eye on his shop that you can't watch over your own!'"

Connecting everything from the outside—taking care of others' business—is a trick that can fool us into feeling we're not alone. Our envy, our quarrels, and our resentments seem to lend us a false sense of control and security. The same thing happens with exaggerated 'love' that wants to live someone else's life. When we discover that taking care of everybody else's business ends up harming our own, we do something about abandoning this trick.

In order for our 'business' to do well, we must understand that this type of external connection will not save us from the feeling of loneliness. To the contrary, it is an illusion that strengthens this feeling.

In order to perceive this connectedness, we must first recover the sense that we are indeed alone. The reality of this world is that the breast which nourishes us is separate from us. Our own mother, our source, or the other who is closest to us all have their independent external destinies.

At the same time, our father—the teacher who we believe will always be at our side, showing us the way—won't be there at the most important times. We will have to make our hardest decisions alone, and it is this discovery that transforms a disciple into a teacher and a child into a parent. No one can do the most important things for you. Yet this sense that we are so profoundly alone does not constitute abandonment. As is the case with everything having to do with spirituality, it is a question of integrating contradictions—being alone makes us discover our connectedness.

> *One of the Baal Shem Tov's students once asked him: 'Why is it that at the most important moments, when we feel a connection with God, we get the impression it was interrupted and that we are once again far away?'*
>
> *The Baal Shem Tov explained: 'When a small child is learning to walk, his father stands in front of him and holds the youngster's two hands so he won't fall. But he soon lets go, and whenever the child gets a little closer, the father moves back a bit. He keeps repeating this over and over until the child learns how to walk.'*

Those moments when we feel this loneliness and lack of connectedness are the moments when we are 'learning to walk'. Once again an apparent contradiction finds spiritual expression in the fact that we are only connected (close) when we are alone. Every other moment, when we feel someone is taking us by the hand, when we have the illusion of being together and safe, we are not walking nor are we being taken care of so that we will learn to walk alone.

This loneliness felt when we are accompanied and connected is something that frees us. It is essential that we learn to tell the difference between the kind of attachment that gradually leads us into isolation and the surrendering of ourselves that sets us on a path which is not ours alone—since many have already passed that way, many still will, and many are already our fellow travelers. This movement that transcends us also places us together and connects us. 'Everything is connected' eventually proves to be a truth (not to be confused with a certainty).

Knowing how to be alone so that we aren't lonely is the secret. The more we try to surround ourselves with people and things, the more isolated we will feel.

> *There is a story about Rabbi Mendel, whose master had just passed away. The rabbi was in anguish over the loss of his teacher. After all, who would be his instructor and tutor from now on? In his despair, he had a dream in which his master tried to comfort him: 'I'm ready to go on being your master!' To which Rabbi Mendel retorted: 'I don't want a master from the other world!'*

Rabbi Mendel carries his master inside himself but the rabbi cannot let go of his absence. The dream forced him to choose between having a 'companion that would make him a lonely man' or being alone but connected. Rabbi Mendel understood what his choices were and by relying on his spiritual intelligence, he decided to reject illusion in favor of something real.

> *True connectedness only exists when we admit we are alone. Most of us fight this fact and consequently feel isolated. The more we are alone, the closer we are to others and to everything.*

Sense of Measure

When more is less

Another important contradiction is found in the notion of measure. We believe that measurements are linear when in fact they really function by saturation. One of the loveliest words in Hebrew is *shiur*, which translates as 'lesson' or 'teaching'. Literally, however, it means 'measure'. There is a precise measure that teaches. And this measure knows how to make perfect use of what is already known, combining it with the exact amount of new knowledge. The proportions of 'what has already been taught' and 'new material' must be determined with utmost precision. A good teacher is an artist who knows how to mix the known and the unknown in a proportion that is the lesson itself. If there's a bit too much of the known and a little less of the unknown—or visa versa—there will be no lesson; instead, the result will be pure repetition, or new information that saturates and does not develop.

If we understand that development requires the right measure, we'll be able to understand a lot about life. All our needs routinely point us to this fact but we resist accepting it. Things are only good if they come in the right measure. More or less always implies some kind of dysfunction or pain. Hunger is a type of pain but so too is nausea brought on by overeating. Nothing that is vital is vital in scarcity or overabundance. Our problem, however, does not lie in understanding this but in understanding how things can be measured.

If we put too much demand on an electrical system and thereby overheat it, its consumption will jump. We will have increased its internal resistance and caused unnecessary losses.

We fail to take this resistance into account and this makes us exceed optimal limits. How many times have we found ourselves in a car, backing up, while we eat a sandwich with one hand and hold a cell phone in the other? We don't realize that the cost of eating, talking on the phone, and backing up is not the same as the sum of doing each of these tasks separately. When we tackle them all together, we run into resistances and built-in costs we don't even usually notice. We think we're saving time but the meter that measures our consumption is simply running faster. There's no question that we're deluding ourselves when we think we're accomplishing more by trying to do several things at the same time.

For everything that is alive, sums turn into more complex equations after they reach a certain level of saturation. Some coefficients increase after a given point. These equations are too complex for us to perceive, and we get fooled. Unfortunately, we only become aware of this when we get sick or when we find ourselves in an irreversible situation that forces us to really stop and assess the reality of these measures.

Shortly after a plane crash, someone asked an air-safety expert: 'Did the pilot make a mistake?' The expert answered: 'One mistake? No, several.' And he explained: 'When a pilot makes a mistake, he leaves a safety area we refer to as 'protocol green' and he enters the yellow warning area. If he makes another mistake, he leaves the yellow protocol for red. From that point on, if he makes one single mistake, his plane will crash.'

I think we can speak about how we manage our lives in quite similar terms. We are not very sensitive when it comes to detecting shifts from the green area into the yellow or red ones. Perhaps, instead of trying to avoid mistakes, it is more important to focus on developing more precise notions about our surrounding reality. These changes in warning levels resemble the changes in saturation levels mentioned earlier.

The built-in cost of higher 'resistances' might seem insignificant when reality shifts from green to yellow. But it is substantial when the change is from yellow to red and irreversible when we reach red. While one plus one equals two in the green area, in the yellow this no longer holds true. In the yellow area, surcharges apply to 'one plus one equals two,' and in the red area, this 'resistance' index may gain such weight that it can turn into a distortion.

An old desert teaching says that when a load threatens to fall off a camel's back, it takes only one person to right it. Once it has fallen, however, four or five people will be needed. This fall means a level of saturation has been reached that alters the scales of impact and consequence. So often in life we find ourselves surprised by these high costs and have no idea where they came from.

Knowing the size of things and understanding the nature of measures is a basic kind of intelligence. Life entails resistances that rise exponentially as we endeavor to wield control over the external world. If you ground yourself in this external world, you'll find your accounts won't balance, because you'll discover excess spending and mysterious costs that don't make sense in terms of your internal accounting. One realm where we feel this most intensely is within the realm of time. The more we try to accomplish in the external world—no matter how rational and cost-effective we are with our time—we'll find ourselves accumulating expenses of the order 'one plus one equals two, and a little change.' This residual amount that brings us to the saturation point can hinder or wreak havoc with many processes in our lives—or even end our lives—if we don't become sensitive to it.

We need to learn that health and balance require the proper measures. Whatever is too much is always more expensive and destructive. But few of us worry about excesses, preferring instead to make scarcity our great villain.

Ethics of Our Fathers, a first-century book of Jewish wisdom, tries to list everything that is costly when in excess (*Pirkei Avot* 2:8). This list of excesses that in fact represent scarcity includes such items as: '*The greater the attachment, the greater the loss; the more the answers, the more the doubts; the more the power, the more the worry.*'

Here the material world is fundamentally different from the spiritual world. Certain measures that can be added together in the material realm actually subtract out in the spiritual realm.

It is said that the Chafetz Chaim once ran into an acquaintance on the street and asked how he was. The man replied: 'Good…but it wouldn't be bad to be better!' To which the Chafetz Chaim commented: 'How do you know it wouldn't be bad?'

Intellectually, we can know that 'more' might not be good but rarely do we have a spiritual understanding that this is true. We go after more, we dream about more, and we trust that this 'more' will bring us satisfaction and well-being. The great irony is that, spiritually speaking, this just isn't true.

Sense of Priority

The order changes the essence

One important teaching found in *Ethics of Our Fathers* (Pirkei Avot 3:11) states that the order of things changes the end result. 'In the name of Rabbi Hanina, it is said that: 'For those for whom reverence precedes wisdom, wisdom shall remain; for those for whom wisdom precedes reverence, wisdom shall not remain.'

What this postulate is telling us is that reverence provides a framework for wisdom. We can't really know something unless we have a clear understanding of the why's, wherefore's, and maybe of the 'who for's'. Reverence is the only firm foundation upon which any interpretation of reality can be grounded. Without it, our knowledge has no meaning, and where there is no meaning, the human being will always try and fill up with whatever meaning he can come up with.

There is a story—about a kind of management issue—that serves as a good illustration of this theory about the order of things changing the outcome.

A master once brought in a metal pail and filled it to the top with large rocks. He asked his disciples: 'Is it full?' They said it was.

He then took some pebbles and dropped them into the pail. Little by little these small stones found their way into the voids left between the big rocks, eventually settling into the bucket. The master once again asked: 'Is it full?' The disciples replied that it was.

The master then took a basin of sand and poured it into the pail. The sand gradually sifted down into the bucket, filling the spaces between the rocks and pebbles and eventually settling as well.

Again the master asked: 'Is it full?' His disciples were certain it was this time.

The master then got a jar full of water and poured it into the bucket. The water quickly found its way into the interstices between the stones and sand.

Now it was indeed full.

So the master asked his disciples what lesson they had gleaned from his demonstration.

One answered that the teaching was meant to show how we can always find more space and that we should be attuned to such opportunities.

The master disagreed. He said: 'The big lesson is that if we don't put the big rocks in first, the pebbles next, then the sand, and last the water, it will be impossible to fit everything in. If we had proceeded in the opposite order, starting with the water, there'd be no room for anything else, especially for the big rocks.'

The water represents physicality—the matter that surrounds everything, even our divine breath. The sand represents the emotional world that permeates our existence; the pebbles are our intellect, which edifies and raises complex structures. The large rocks are the foundation stones of reverence. If we don't put them in first, there'll never be any place for them. Our bucket can only hold everything if we put reverence before all else.

It's easier for us to understand this when we substitute reverence with ethics. If an ethical motivation does not underlie our initial impetus, our original intention, then we will never find room for it later.

Some priorities can have nothing else placed in front of them.

Some priorities must come before all others.

Remember the saying of the Rebbe of Kotzk that *'the most important thing for me is whatever I am doing at the moment!'*

The order changes the final outcome, especially if we don't begin with the here and now. If our now comes before the past and the future, then our spiritual intelligence is manifesting itself. If, on the other hand, the past or future take priority over the here and now, spiritual intelligence is impossible.

The first step is always to combine reverence with the here and now. This is the raw material of presence and of spiritual intelligence. By joining the present moment and reverence, we react to life spontaneously, with great drive and yet with humility.

Who among us has never felt the wit and vitality of an answer or an attitude that sprang from a present moment, from a given 'now'? Such experiences—when we rely on reverence to ground us in the true freedom of the here and now—are always exhilarating and magic.

If we are to enjoy a good quality of life and be eminently free, not needing to resort to guilt mechanisms or finger-pointing, then we depend upon the grace of reverence. It prioritizes 'fear' instead of 'fright'. And fear, which acts like large rocks, should come before any other content.

Sense of Resource

If you have a lot of yourself, you have everything

One of the most important discoveries for anyone takes part intensively in life is the sense of resource. It is perhaps one of the hardest senses to develop since it feeds on our frustrations, losses, and needs. There is a marvelous flip side to the feeling of surprise and wonder we experience when we discover the universe has conceived of a breast to fit our famished mouths: for everything we lack or need, there is a way to deal with it. We can find relief for everything that goes wrong, for all pain, all suffering, and all failures. Death itself is the most remarkable proof that resources exist for all living things—for death is a way out, even if no one is eager to use this option. But we should realize death is nevertheless a resource—perhaps the greatest proof that there is a resource for everything. Even when we don't know how to deal with violence or with critical needs, there is always the option of fainting, blacking out, or dying.

People usually think of death as an aberration, as a symbol that life has no resources. Yet it is just the opposite. There's no problem, trouble, or hardship for which resources do not exist, precisely because we can always count on the end. Unfortunately, this knowledge seems only to be used by those who are suffering so much that they find in death the ultimate demonstration of the universe's mercy. There is a way out even when there's no way out, thanks to death.

We can't begin to fathom the complexity entailed in producing the mechanisms of death and detachment. The same force that produced breasts took the trouble to create death as the last resource. In other words, life begins with the resource of the breast and ends with the resource of death.

It is extremely hard for us to understand that a human being's education and preparation for life depend upon scarcity, absences, unmet needs, and frustrations. Pain and suffering have always served as resources to help us grow, develop, and reach our objectives. The hunt begins with a pain—the pain of hunger. This pain is a resource. Without it, survival would be impossible. But a baby doesn't see hunger as the origin of the possibility of satisfying this hunger; quite the contrary, it sees hunger as the origin of discontentment and unfulfilled wants. Like children whose palates have been spoiled by too much ketchup, we ignore countless spices because we can't recognize any taste unless it's sweet. Bitterness, tartness, spiciness, and so many other flavors are wonderful resources but if your palate only finds pleasure in sweetness, it will never enjoy the others.

Anything that happens to us presents us with resources. Our disbelief in this fact is generally expressed in the words 'And now?' But 'now' always has a resource. And this is our ultimate hope and source of faith: when things don't go the way we want, whatever happens, we can always count on resources that will help us deal with life. This is the very definition of life and what makes life so fascinating and dear to us. None of us wants to give up a reality that does everything for us: it causes us to be born, it shows us how to grow up, and it grants us the mercy of the final ending.

To many people this may sound like resignation or an abandonment of life, but it isn't. Borderline to resignation lies acceptance, and the fine line separating the two makes all the difference in the world.

One of the most well-known tales from Jewish folklore tells of a very poor and desperate man who went to see his rabbi. He tells the rabbi he can't stand the way his family lives anymore. He has ten children and they all share a tiny one-room shack. The man says he's going crazy, with children all over the place and no room to breathe. He has no privacy with his wife, and everyone's quality of life is intolerable.

The rabbi listens intently to all the man's troubles and then asks him: 'By any chance do you own a cow?'

'A cow?' the man asks, not understanding where the rabbi is going. 'Yes, we have a cow that gives us milk and cream and such!'

'Very well. Here's what you're going to do...' the rabbi declares firmly. 'Take the cow and put it inside your house. Keep her there for a week and then come back.'

Incredulous, the man obeys, more because of the rabbi's great prestige as a holy man than for any other reason. A week later, he comes back in even greater despair. Dark circles mark his eyes, his clothes are filthy, and his wretched appearance stirs pity.

'How are you?' the rabbi asks, paying scant attention to the poor man's pathetic state.

'How am I? The last thing I needed was that cow relieving itself on my floor and taking up what little space we had!

'Very well... So take the cow out now and come back in a week,' the rabbi says in a tone of wisdom.

When the week ends, the man comes back unrecognizable. He looks rested and elated. The rabbi asks: 'How's everything going?'

'I've never been better. Ever since the day that cow left, our life has changed. There's room for everyone and we've discovered how spacious our home is!'

Told by grandparents to grandchildren, this story conveys a message that is very often poorly understood. It's not only about appreciating our human ability to resign ourselves whenever we come up against a situation worse than our previous one. This trick has to do with how we look at the 'full half glass,' and it is of very limited efficaciousness. After all, there are real situations where the level in the glass can drop well below half, in an infinite spiral of ever worsening situations. Life is not enjoyable because it could always be worse—life is enjoyable whenever we realize we can avail ourselves of resources appropriate to each moment and situation. There are resources for living well in a tiny house filled with many children. The possibility that things could be worse awakens us to resources that were always available but of which we were unaware.

This kind of discovery is common among the sick. But in this situation too it is possible to misunderstand the notion. The idea that

'I was happy and didn't know it' can be an illusion that leaves us stuck dreaming about what no longer is. What the story of the cow really tells us is that we can always discover the resources at hand. If a sick person can perceive resources of pleasure and happiness that he didn't see before, this discovery should help him to not miss things of the past but instead to seek out all the resources already available in his present moment that he hasn't yet managed to access.

Resigning yourself means relinquishing and abandoning things. It means settling for a perceived lack of resources. Faith is the opposite of resignation; it's about facing up to things. It means we are not resigned, because we know there are resources for each given situation and moment. We refuse to resign ourselves to a given situation precisely because we aren't finding the resources but we are not giving up the search. We so often confuse faith with escaping, when it's really about struggling, about a vital effort to keep from losing our focus on the fact that life is always, by definition, about the existence of resources. Despair comes when we lose hope that these resources exist.

Lending someone a hand is always about helping them find another way to perceive the existence of these resources. One of the rabbis' wisest recommendations concerns how to help someone who is carrying a burden. They warn us about the danger of wanting to remove someone else's burden. We don't know what this burden means for that person. Of course we should be alert to any kind of assistance we might be able to offer. We can help bear the burden for a few moments, we can arrange things so the burden isn't so unwieldy, but we can't take someone else's burden away. This is something only that person can do. And it's all about resources.

Whenever we remove someone else's burden, we're depriving that individual of the chance to discover what resources are available to whomever bears such a load. Unfortunately, we often do this with our own children. Because of our love for them, we get rid of obstacles and burdens that would serve the wonderful role of inciting them to discover resources. They are momentarily immune to the problem or hardship facing them but they are also robbed of life's prime asset, which is faith in resources. Life becomes nothing more than the breast we can draw nourishment from while all else lies outside of life and becomes a reason for losing hope and giving ourselves over to despair. They miss the chance to acquire the fundamental ability to realize that hunger and discomfort are never permanent. All suffering is a kind of disturbance or imbalance that leads us to some kind of resource. Even if this is death— the ultimate resource.

There's an anecdote about a rabbi who came before his community and announced in a somber tone:

> *'I've got three pieces of news for you. One's good, the other's bad, and the third is in between. In what order would you like me to tell them?'*
>
> *The community immediately asked him to tell them the bad news first.*
>
> *'The bad news,' the apologetic rabbi said, 'is that the roof of our synagogue is in risk of collapsing and we'll need formidable resources to fix it.'*
>
> *A sour 'oh!' went up from the community.*
>
> *'The good news, however,' the rabbi went on in a tone of relief, 'is that we already have these resources.'*
>
> *Another 'oh!' was heard, this time a mixture of jubilation and satisfaction.*
>
> *'The in-between news is that these resources are in your pockets!'*

This is our true relationship with any kind of needed resources. Reality forces us to face an amazing gamut of trials and tribulations. For each piece of 'bad news' we hear comes the 'good news' that resources are already available. Of course our intelligence lies in our being able to handle the 'in-between' news. In this story, the pocket symbolizes a place of possibility but also of loss. It represents everything we don't want to give up, but which would make us see the resources.

In order for us to utilize these needed resources, we must rely upon the faith we acquired from our experience with those burdens that were not artificially removed, burdens that induced us to find solutions and ways out.

Faith is the 'in-between' news, although many religious traditions tell us faith is all about the 'Good News'. Such good news can contain illusion and alienation. Bad news leaves us desperate, good news leaves us resigned, while the 'in-between' news endows us with faith.

Any messiah who brings only good news is a false messiah. All religious traditions that propose to remove burdens lead us to disappointment and despair. Only messiahs and traditions that bring us 'in-between' news subscribe to the intelligent dimension of spirituality.

In-between news is inevitably not about removing burdens but about realizing they play a role. When you remove a burden, you must pay a price but you will also be able to rely on the resources inherent to this burden. Removing burdens any other way is the same as throwing the baby out with the bath water.

By recovering our burdens as our own and learning to appreciate them—even though they do not represent good news but something more like in-between news—we obtain our allotment and our very lives. And whoever has a lot of himself has it all.

> *Whoever has a lot of himself—not just the sweet tastes but the whole array of life's wonderful spices, even the bitter—will develop a sense of resource and will have everything. By taking hold of our lives and claiming responsibility for them, the resource of resources is made available to us, that is, faith in the existence of resources.*

Sense of Mission

Our garbage and vices make us unique

One of the most common fantasies in the realm of spirituality is the notion that we have a mission to discover. Several forms of spiritual ignorance take advantage of this illusion by offering the ego a refuge in a specific religion or sect. Religiosity often serves to help us recover our self-esteem. There's nothing wrong with this role, as long as we don't confuse it with the true purposes of spirituality.

It is not at all unusual for people to think they are recovering their spirituality because someone tells them they are 'sensitive' or a 'medium' and they should develop this potential. Perhaps these individuals draw some benefit from recalling moments in their lives when they were more aware of and in closer touch with this dimension and this way of reading reality. But unfortunately, what most often happens is that the individual recovers the illusion that he or she has a mission. Such people are visited by thoughts like 'I have to do something; there's something special I must do in this world. I, and no one else, can accomplish this task.' There is malice in inducing such thinking: it is a half-truth (and perhaps spiritual ignorance uses this as one of its most frequent 'brainwashing' techniques). Yes, we do have a mission that makes us unique but it has nothing to do with the notion of 'I.' As we have seen earlier, self-esteem is healthy when it is about 'who we are' but never when it is about 'what we are.'

Missions lend us a title and imbue us with a unique task. Illusion! There is nothing we can do that is unique, save one thing. We are indeed unique in this universe, but again this has to do with 'being' and never with 'doing'; we are all replaceable, from the coarsest person to the most refined and sensitive. Our leaders, prophets, and even messiahs, no matter how great their merit, are all playing roles, and what lends them their immortality is the space they occupy; whether we like it or not, this space could always be filled by someone else.

This sense of mission is a trick we often fall back on when facing a life crisis. The Rabbi of Berdichev said: 'We must be wary of arrogance and pride, for they require no solid basis. A person can be lying in a bed, shivering with cold under a tattered blanket, and still think: 'I am very special, I am great!" Every person is special for who he or she is—but for what he or she is, no one is special, although that is how we all perceive ourselves.

Spirituality offers us a great contradiction: it teaches us we are only special because of what we do about our *shmutz*—our garbage, our shadows, our vices. Our flaws are what best define our mission. Focusing our attention on the things we should get right (to the extent possible for us)—here is an exclusive mission. In this sense we are unique; the issues we need to resolve are what make us special and singular.

Most people prefer to ask themselves what they can give the world or what great contribution they are meant to leave humanity; rarely do they realize their unique role is to repair themselves, to get themselves right. It's easier to put up with your own 'dirty diapers' than go to the trouble of taking them off and cleaning yourself. But missions are more about changing diapers than about dreams of a pure and fragrant world. We can do nothing more practical towards saving the world than changing our own diapers.

But what glory lies in this? If glory is about doing something unique, then this is the only glorious task within our reach. The way we look at famous people who have made a difference—a look of envy, accompanied by the wishful thought 'If only I could trade places with her!'—is an illusion that, like all others, leads to dissatisfaction.

> *Rabbi Bunem once said:*
> *'I would not like to trade places with the patriarch Abraham. How would it be better for God if Abraham were the blind Bunem and the*

blind Bunem were Abraham? Instead of hoping for this to happen, I think I'd better try to grow a little beyond who I am today!'

Going through our garbage is the holiest task and the only task that affords any real gain in this universe. In English, when we want to call attention to someone's arrogance and pride, we say 'He is full of himself.' Portuguese has a maxim that spells out this contradiction in quite concrete terms: 'He has the king in his belly.' This phrase reminds us of what lies in the belly: our digestive tract and our feces. Is this your 'king'? Don't forget that you are a 'vessel of filth'. Indeed, that is what it's all about. Your kingdom is your garbage. Dealing with your limitations and your vices will make you a king, unique. No one can be a king except through their capacity to transform themselves and correct their imperfections.

It should be pointed out that this is the most efficient way to achieve growth in any situation. In business management, for example, before seeking to improve performance by expanding outward, steps should be taken against inner inefficiency and incompetence. Eliminating these will be enough to bring real growth in resources.

Of all forms of pride and arrogance, the worst are those displayed by people who consider themselves pious or spiritual prodigies. We are never swimming harder against the tide of spirituality or displaying as much ignorance as when we feel responsible for an external mission, one outside ourselves. We fulfill our true missions without knowing they are missions, when we turn our attention to ourselves and make ourselves grow beyond who we are today.

Sense of Illness

Recognizing what takes you where you don't want to go

We can summarize then that our physical instincts rely on fear to help us avoid danger; our emotional instincts rely on distrust to steer us away from emotional dangers; our intellectual instincts rely order to avoid confusion and incoherence; while spirituality recognizes danger in a specific way, namely— realizing that we 'aren't going where we want to.'

Spiritual ignorance always seeks to project dangers onto external, satanic temptations, as we saw in the question of exorcism. But the only external 'evil' is inevitable and should therefore lie beyond the realm of our concerns. The real danger lies in a web we weave ourselves. It is our inner voices that tempt us and that keep us from following the course we really want to take. There is no compass other than the realization that we are headed where we don't want to go. There are maps, like the Scriptures and the teachings, but you have to know where you are, where you want to go, and how to get there by the path of least resistance. In other words, there is no instruction manual. And even maps must be constantly updated to include the changes that occur over time.

In the Biblical text, when Moses asks God His name, he hears this answer: 'I shall be what I shall be.' peculiar way of defining or naming oneself lets us understand that God is the absolute force that in its wholeness manages To Be what it proposes to be. Everything and everyone else manage to be what they truly propose to be only in part. We are taken where we don't want to go, and perhaps this is the definition of the Evil Impulse that appears in rabbinic literature, like a kind of satanic manifestation within ourselves. This internal trickery we play upon ourselves demands that each of us know our own style of self-illusion.

The following quotation from *Ethics of Our Fathers* (Pirkei Avot 2:6) points out problems that affect spirituality and its origin: '*A brutish man cannot fear sin; an ignorant man cannot be pious; nor can the shy man learn, or the impatient man teach.*'

According to this teaching, insensitivity, ignorance, avoidance, shame and impatience are behaviors that make us spiritually ill. There is no human trouble that can't be broken down into components of these four factors, which as symptoms suggest certain diagnoses or prognoses.

First of all, refinement is what allows us to tolerate contradictions. Through it we learn not to generalize but to appreciate diversity and surprise. Seeing only black and white, the brute becomes color-blind to life. In black and white, all contradictions appear to be incoherent or mistakes. If we don't pay attention to nuances, the only sense that will make sense is disbelief and cynicism.

Avoidance is an attitude we use in order to evade confrontation with our own limitations. Since the greatest limitation of all is death, the person that avoids is someone who is so afraid of death that he simply settles. A landless man clinging to the land or a lifeless man clinging to life, the person that constantly avoids becomes insensitive to all weaknesses or limitations. Unless we understand our pettiness and our own restrictions, we're unable to see our neighbor, the other, as an equal, nor will we be able to develop compassion. And when compassion is not present, lack of responsibility will be the perverse outcome. As the word itself says, responsibility has to do with the ability to be responsive. We can only respond to life and to the other if we respond to ourselves. Indifference to violence or to someone else's suffering is a derivative of our spiritual stagnation and avoidance.

Shame keeps us from growing. Shame can be a positive feeling when applied to our behavior but not when applied to our person. Being ashamed of something I've done is quite different from being ashamed of who I am. Someone who is ashamed of himself does not ask questions and does not leave himself open. And nothing is more important for spiritual intelligence than recognizing that we aren't what we have done; we are what we do. Others can judge the past, but we always have the chance to change, at any instance of our lives. At any given moment there's always some way to keep from feeling ashamed of ourselves—often thanks to our very ability to feel ashamed of what we've done. What I'm saying is that shame keeps us from being present; instead, it forever is taking us back into a past that points an accusing finger at us. Shame does not allow the present to take advantage of its finest feature: being the solvent of the past.

Someone who is ashamed has trouble learning not just because he's unable to ask questions. Since he's always worried about unsettled matters form the past, he is unable to be present, and this is the first prerequisite for learning. Reb Pinchas once stated: 'We are always, constantly, being taught by life. And why then do we have so much trouble learning? Because life teaches but it doesn't repeat!'

He who is ashamed lets countless opportunities in life pass him by, simply because he is hiding rather than being present.

Lastly, impatience reflects an erroneous understanding of life, based on the notion that something more interesting and enjoyable is always going to come. Later is always more important than now. However remember that 'The most important thing is whatever you are doing at the moment.'

We simply can't imagine how it would alter the quality of our lives if we could make what we are doing the most important thing. The ensuing pleasure we would experience and the quality of everything we did would suffice to make us happy. The impatient person inside us all doesn't know that the greatest happiness consists simply of realizing that whatever we are doing, at any given moment, is the most important thing.

These symptoms very often appear together. Stop and think how many people you know who are insensitive and who are also to some degree avoiding, ashamed or impatient.

Sense of Blessing

Dedication to life, not to immortality

What is a blessing?

To bless is, first and foremost, to pay attention. And not just pay attention but pay attention as closely as possible. We don't realize it but whenever someone's attention is focused enough and precise enough, it becomes a blessing. Great spiritual masters and leaders have incredible influence on us exactly because they are able to identify our deepest wants and needs. They pay radical attention to us, thereby uncovering the heart of whatever is most critical for each one of us. And by expressing their desire that our needs be met, they bless us. Anyone who can pay very close attention to others is able to bless, and anyone who can pay radically close attention to him or herself will feel blessed.

The state of blessedness is being fully present in the here and now. Any expectation that extrapolates life's boundaries at the moment when life is taking place displaces /* removes us from the state of blessedness. This is why blessedness comes easy to us during big events in our lives, such as marriages or good-byes. Whatever is routine usually removes /* displaces us from the state of blessedness because by definition it involves a time when our expectations lie elsewhere. We are not radically present in things that are routine. Routine life always entails some degree of automatic behavior, when we are easily seduced by fantasies, precisely because what is routine is so fragile. In other words, what is routine deprives us of a sense of blessing because it does not require the minimum amount of attention necessary to produce this blessing.

The kind of intelligence portrayed in the Bible—particularly in the Pentateuch—is unmistakable in the only blessing taught directly by the Creator. Known as the blessing of Aharon, or the Priestly Blessing, these verses are in fact a manual on blessings.

The text reads (Num. 5:24-26):

> *The Lord bless thee, and keep thee.*
> *The Lord make his face shine upon thee and be gracious unto thee.*
> *The Lord lift up his countenance upon thee, and give thee peace.*

This blessing encompasses three essential areas of our needs. 'Bless' refers to concerns of a physical nature; 'shine,' to intellectual concerns; and 'countenance,' to emotional concerns. While prosperity, intelligence, and emotions encompass all our needs, they themselves do not constitute blessings.

If we stop to think about it carefully, we'll realize that each of these areas must be covered in order for it to involve a true blessing. The concept 'and keep you' is linked to the idea of 'progress' (blessing); 'and be gracious to you' is linked to 'intelligence' ('shine upon you'); 'and give you peace' is linked to 'affection' (attention). Neither prosperity nor intelligence nor even affection are measures, as we saw earlier. Too much of them can causes as much suffering and imbalance as too little.

If we are to enjoy prosperity, we must be 'kept' or protected from it. Unless we know the value of things, nothing can be transformed into prosperity. Being blessed is not merely a question of enjoying the availability of an asset but of possessing the attention needed to know what to do with this wealth. Unless we use our attention to understand the true value of material goods, they can entice us into attachment and frivolity.

At the same time, if the Creator is to shine upon us, intelligence and creativity are not enough. 'Grace' is an interesting measure because it puts intelligence or cleverness to its final test. When we fail to use our intelligence honestly and spontaneously, or when we use it with disguised or false purposes, there is nothing graceful about us. Our being filled with grace is thus a quality that defines the limits of intelligence, either transforming it into wisdom or, contrarily, into cleverness that harbors malice. By paying attention to the world around us and to ourselves, we are illuminated with good sense. What lends intelligence the quality of blessedness is its relevance and propriety.

Lastly, attention and affection may or may not be synonymous with blessedness. Too much love or the exaggerated devotion of a mother or dear one can often disturb us. It is only when this attention is expressed in an appropriate degree that it produces peace. Think about a person who out of devotion meddles in someone else's life or about a lover who out of affection becomes jealous and possessive. This will inarguably put an end to our peace. In other words, even affection is only a blessing when we receive it in a degree that does not jeopardize our peace.

The sense of blessing is a toast to life; it is the recognition—thanks to sharp attention—of that which each moment lays before us. This toast can only be raised when we relinquish our expectation of immortality. Indeed, life and immortality are antonyms. When we try to clutch life and control it, hoping to achieve the sensation we are immortal, life will elude us. Immortality barters the present in exchange for future expectations. In order to ensure it won't die, immortality relinquishes the here and now. After all, does not death present itself to life at each and every moment? As long as life and death are present, blessedness is possible. It is our desire for immortality that voids any chance of blessing. This is because the wish for immortality represents a distraction—the absence of attention that cannot bless.

Sense of Salvation

The opposite of pleasure is not pain but comfort

Blessing is to attention as salvation is to risk.

Our common sense tells us being blessed means we can live detached and disinterested, wallowing in comfortable alienation. But we have just defined blessedness as swimming against the tide of this perception. We run into the same thing when we nourish the expectation that we will be rescued and saved from a world whose uncertainties make it seem hostile. After all, the biggest wish of someone who seeks to control the world around him is that some day he'll enjoy the tranquility that only absolute security can bring. This is the only way he can take a vacation from the stress occasioned by an existence based on feeling we should reach some imaginary end and move through life racking up equally imaginary successes.

The peace we aspire to attain through control can only be found if we live with risk and uncertainty. We like to imagine that our mother's uterus was a place of total comfort, the source of our feelings of tenderness and gentleness. But if there is something this place was not is comfortable. The mother who compresses her fetus as she sleeps, along with the uterine environment itself—a place of gases, acidity, and other discomforts—translate into a reality that is everything but comfortable. The womb is undoubtedly a place of great pleasure but of pain as well. In point of fact, it is only a place of pleasure because of the pain it also holds.

There is no pleasure that is not linked to a situation of pain. Sexuality leads to the pain of childbirth; eating leads to the fermentation, digestion, and defecation of food; in order to accomplish our tasks, we must expend effort and struggle; and so on and so forth. Someone who wants to achieve control is not worried first and foremost about pleasure but about how to deal with pain. As a result, he seeks a comfort that, in doing away with pain, also does away with the possibility of pleasure—and is in any case a trick fated to fail. Because not only is it impossible to avoid pain forever, but living without pleasure is the opposite of being saved.

We need to accept the words painted on the back of a trucker's vehicle: 'Life is like driving at night: you can only see as far as your headlights but you can do it your whole trip.' We don't need to see from one city to the next in order to make our journey a safe one.

The consequences of this search for comfort are felt not just at an individual level. Our twenty-first-century society shows all the symptoms of a civilization that reduces pain by endeavoring to attain comfort and control but that concomitantly reduces pleasure—a pleasure that should be reflected in little things, like demonstrating solidarity with our neighbor or simply making contact with someone else. If we are 'comfortable', the world around us can fall apart without it upsetting us. When we are comfortable—that is, when we feel risks are farther away—we identify less with our neighbor and his or her pains (and pleasures).

The archetypical Biblical figure who represents this way of thinking is Noah. His name in Hebrew (*Noach*) literally means 'he who is comfortable.' When God informs Noah that He's going to destroy the world but that Noah will be saved, the man doesn't even blink. As long as he's safe and sound, everything's fine. He starts building his little ark, just like we who believe that in our little world, in our home, as long as we're fine, what's going on in the rest of the world matters little to us. Instead of taking action to help other living creatures—as other Biblical figures would (Abraham and Moses, for example)—Noah keeps comfortably quiet.

Noah's similarity to the good citizens of our twenty-first-century globalized world goes beyond mere indifference. Like today, Noah was politically correct. Saving one pair of each species shows a concern similar to ours today, when we try to save the whales and the dolphins—

while letting millions of people die of poverty in Africa or on the corner of our street. In his time and society, it was enough for Noah to be only politically correct. Being correct has become unnecessary—or even foolish—just as long as we are 'politically correct.'

Spiritual ignorance lies in pursuing a comfort that avoids pain at the cost of blocking our access to pleasure. We trade pleasure for entertainment, for things that make us depart from our reality and move away from ourselves. In the medium run, the price of this kind of escape is depression and despair.

Headlights that won't let us see farther down the road than just ahead of us offer a way of seeing ourselves in the dark. There is light, but light that interacts with darkness, affording us an efficacious way to reach our destination even in the midst of insecurity and the unknown. It is the comfort of wanting to light everything down to the end of the road that produces true blindness. This view of our arrival replaces the essence of the journey—a journey made of blessing-attention and of pleasure-risk, without which there is no salvation.

Spirituality Does Not Exist

As we saw earlier, a blessing is made up of precise measures that satisfy without glutting. Moreover, these components manifest themselves in three areas: the physical, the emotional, and the intellectual. So we are missing the fourth dimension we started to analyze: the spiritual dimension. Where is it to be found? What is a spiritual blessing? What is the part of us or the organ that benefits from spiritual blessings, pleasures, or delights? It looks like it doesn't exist.

Rabbi Bunem used to say: *'He who has much study becomes an unbeliever and a heretic; he who gives himself over to love becomes fickle and lascivious; he who is disciplined becomes egotistical and rigid. So if study, love, and discipline yield these results, what characterizes a good person?'* *Rabbi Bunem thus finished his thought: 'All three things together!'*

What Rabbi Bunem is saying is that there is a measure of measures, which is what the Biblical blessing also teaches. Just as there is a precise measure for physical, emotional, and intellectual blessings, so is there an ideal situation in which these measures exist all together. The three of these areas in balance produce another balance, another measure of measures themselves—which is absolute or spiritual blessing.

In other words, spirituality comes from the combination of physical, emotional, and intellectual well-being. It is therefore the expression of all human potentiality in appropriate measure, not too little and not much. These moments of harmony allow us to grasp spirituality.

In this regard, one of the most amazing ritual objects are the phylacteries (*tefilin*), which most likely originated in ancient Egypt and are used by Jews down through today. Made of strips of leather and small boxes containing bits of parchment on which Biblical verses have been written, these objects are placed by Jews on one of their arms and on the head once a day, preferably in the morning. Symbolically, they link or tie together the arm, the heart, and the head. In so doing, they become an object of spirituality as they manifest the wish that the day begin with the union of these three vital elements: doing, feeling, and thinking. If we manage to create 'communicative channels' between these three spheres, the result of all we do will be that which 'we wish would be,' and we become the image and likeness of a Creator who is the force that names itself *'I will be that I will be'*. In other words, if I am whole, integrated and full, then my history and my future will be reflections of myself. I am therefore a manifestation, on a smaller scale, of that which created me.

Any expression of only one or two legs of this tripod of human existence will result in aberrations and deformation. Reb Bunem left us a list of the deviations that might occur when one of these three areas rules. But neither do they represent us in pairs. Intellect and emotions alone will yield inaction and alienation; deeds and intellect alone will yield psychopathic behavior and cruelty; and deeds and emotion alone will yield injustice and fickleness.

Spirituality is this ability to be ourselves. We often believe that the three dimensions of our existence—the physical, emotional, and intellectual—are mutually independent. But that is not a fact. They must relate to each other in an integrated and not compensatory fashion. If, for example, we are not well developed on a physical level, we try to make up for it intellectually, or visa versa; if our emotional level is not adequately developed, we endeavor to compensate intellectually, or visa versa; and so on. These imbalances derived from our effort to overcompensate what is missing in a different sphere are the source of our organic, somatic, and psychic illnesses.

What messes us up most in this mismanagement of our selves is the fact that we are dealing with a tripod. Spiritually, the way animals work is much simpler—they only have to deal with the physical and the emotional. It's much less complicated for an irrational animal to be blessed.

Our animal structure likewise induces us to try to work by pairing dimensions. Combinations of each two give life to specific skills. Our intellectual and physical spheres interact to produce speech. Our emotional and physical spheres interact to produce gestures, faces, or what we now call body language. And our intellect and emotions produce thought.

We must make an effort to render such expressions representative of our tripods. We must make an effort if we are to bring emotion into our speech; we must make an effort to bring intelligence to our posture; and we must make an effort to bring action to our thoughts. The first effort yields sincerity; the second, justice; and the last, ethics. Honesty, justice, and solidarity are in fact the tripod sustains the spiritual workings of religious traditions

Actually, this spirituality that does not exist—because it is merely the interaction of three other abilities that do indeed exist—is called 'lower spirituality' in mystical Judaism. According to this line of thought, there is another spirituality—a 'higher' spirituality—which exists independently, unrelated to the orchestrated workings of expressions that we perceive to be real and existent.

The Ultimate Contradiction:

The Difference That Makes Us The Same

Perhaps the most amazing thing about spirituality is that it alone has produced only one single term that is unique to it. Only one word belongs solely to the realm of spirituality, and most people have trouble understanding this term, even though they use it all the time. I'm referring to the word and concept 'holy'.

In the Biblical text, the Creator makes a point of identifying this word with spirituality's greatest task: 'And ye shall be holy, for I am holy' (Lev. 11:44). What is meant by 'be holy'? In archaic Hebrew, the root of the word—*k_d_sh*— means 'to set aside' or 'to separate.'

As described in the Biblical text, the main feature of the Creation is separation. According to the text, transformational, creational power lies in the act of separating and differentiating. The heavens are separated from the earth, light from darkness, seas from land, animals from each other, and the human being from animals. Difference not only creates. It would also appear to maintain life, since today we know that biodiversity is essential to the balance and preservation of our environment. And it doesn't seem to be a matter solely of collective differences or differences between species. Differences between individuals are a sign of health, as modern genetics is showing us. The reproduction of like beings impoverishes life so greatly that it jeopardizes it. At each act of procreation, diversity among living things engenders an act of creation of something different.

With today's possibility of creating genetically identical beings, we face the possibility of creating beings without spirit. This is because the greatest feature of this invisible facet of life is difference itself, or the possibility of being holy. Having a spirit means holding inside a piece of an infinite jigsaw puzzle, where the prerequisite for being part of the whole is having a difference that fits in with all the other differences.

The key characteristic of this difference is that it binds together instead of separating. It is what makes us belong to the whole. We have here another sacred contradiction: in order to be a part, we must be different. Or to put it better, what unites us is not equality but difference itself. It is through difference that the Creator exists within us; it is this difference that is the likeness among all of us and also between us and the Creator. It is this very difference that is the transcending element within each one of us. The sign of our singularity is the spirit breathed into each one of us, as if we were all, individually, like Adam. Rather than being insufflated with breath-soul, we are insufflated with difference.

Thus is holiness planted in us. We are set apart, made differently, so that we may exist and identify ourselves with all that is solitary in its difference. Our sadness in not finding a mate only vanishes when we encounter someone truly different who is therefore like us.

In this sense, spirituality is the ongoing mimesis of this condition, with the purpose of soothing the discomfort brought on because we feel separated and lonely. Transcending this means carrying out rituals or living moments that make us recall or put us in touch with this feeling of closeness, but always by way of difference. Equality pushes us apart and dehumanizes us, or, to put it more precisely, it rips out our spirit.

Hallowing or making holy involves making something become distinct. Setting aside a special day, distinct from all others, as the Creator did with the Sabbath, is a way of teaching us human beings the secret of not being alone in this universe. Differentiate, and you will find a sacred peace, an encounter with an essence that is yours.

This mechanism for fostering encounters is the basic idea behind the ancient Temple of Jerusalem, which is probably the model for all the temples that have ever existed, that exist today, and that will exist in the future. As in a science-fiction scene, the creatures discovered a form of connection with their Creator. Simple to beget but hard to comprehend, the Temple of de Jerusalem created concepts of difference, of holiness.

There was a nation different from others; in it stood a city different from others; and in it was a mount different from others. On this mount, there was a place—a temple—wherein there existed a place different from other places and which was called 'holy of holies.' Priests who were members of a tribe that was different from other tribes took care of this temple, and within this tribe were members of a specific family that was different from other families in the tribe. And in this temple, people celebrated days that were different from other days. A different place, in a different time, in a different human being—this is the antenna that makes contact with a broad and profound universe feasible.

This is the biggest challenge for spiritual traditions. On the one hand, they must ethically reflect that human beings are equal, yet at the same time they must underscore their difference, so that they can be truly equal. For this reason religions sometimes lose themselves in the notion that they are different, and they kill, while at other times they lose themselves in the idea that they are equal, and they are sapped of their spiritual power.

> *There is a story about a young boy who used to hide in the woods every day after school. One day his father asked him what he was doing while hidden in the woods every day. 'Me... I talk with God,' the boy replied. 'But my son,' came the father's reaction, 'don't you know that God is everywhere? You don't need to go into the woods to talk with God. He's the same whether you talk with him here at home or in the woods!' 'Of course God is the same, Dad,' the boy calmly replied. 'But I'm not the same!'*

We seek out difference in traditions and temples not because God is different but because we are different. And only through this difference does the spirit momentarily become real for us. On the basis of these fleeting moments we become transcendent and we join together in difference with all that is different. The subtle distinction between making sacred and making separate is the finely tuned harmony that distinguishes between intelligent spirituality and spiritual ignorance.

This is always the danger with spiritual manifestations. How can we keep the deliberate act of 'setting apart' or 'separating' in rituals from fostering separation instead of holiness? Separation is not a difference that fosters communion. To the contrary, it is celebration of the ego and not of the spirit.

Perhaps we could say that the spirit is what is different about us and what makes us equal. The ego, on the other hand, is what is equal in all of us and differentiates us.

The truth of the matter is that spirituality speaks of things that have no manifestation but that are behind all manifestations. Intelligence lies not only in recognizing this subtlety but in changing our models of understanding and functioning in our lives. It is about allowing ourselves to delegate greater power to our senses so that they will lead us not necessarily to success or triumph but to well being.

Peace lies in our being so profoundly different quieting our inner fire to honor our potentials, which are distinct—while at the same time being so profoundly equal— quieting our consciousness.

This integration is sacred. It is sacred because it sets us apart, if not within the absolute universe then within the universe we know. Encounters are the key goal of all intelligence, as we saw earlier. Our intelligence serves no other purpose than to re-encounter the path that will take us back to the 'garden' from which we originate.

Long ago, when we made use of the Tree of Knowledge and set off on a final journey, we discovered exile. Our only tool for survival became the wisdom for which we lost our way home. But this is a mistaken idea. We in fact have two tools: the wisdom with which we left and a deep desire to return and to re-encounter. Without the latter, the former will take us farther. This 'farther' might seem to be an achievement but it really makes us more lost.

Like the story mentioned earlier about the man lost in the forest. When he finally sees the light of a lantern, he discovers the lantern is held by a blind man who is as lost as he is. Frustrated, he thinks he has gained nothing from this encounter, nothing that can give him hope. But he is sorely mistaken. The blind man doesn't need to see the way out; for the blind man, the feeling of being in a forest or of being lost in the middle of nowhere, simply don't exist.

The light of his lantern, of no use whatsoever to him, is essential if the other is to see him. The light's purpose is to draw those who have trouble with not seeing and to teach them a peacefulness that their vision does not afford them. Their ability to 'see' throws them into despair because they are so deeply lost and don't know their way out. Together, the two men have greater resources, or perhaps all the resources. The one who can't see creates lights for the one who can, so that he will know the peace of blindness.

Using sight to foster encounters with that which doesn't see is our great resource. As the rooster cannot see but knows how to distinguish day from night, we come to realize that darkness is nothing else than anxiety and despair. And the blind man's idea is indeed efficient. Light as many lanterns as you can so that others may find you, but the secret is that they are not to be used to find your way out. The way out only makes itself revealed to those who have grown used to the darkness. For those who are accustomed to shadows have no trouble making out the forms that lie in the dark.

And the forest becomes home; and exile ends with the meeting of the exiled. And whoever keeps looking for the way out with a lantern won't see any of this.

The Clarity of Darkness

Going the wrong way there's always a light that up until that point lay in darkness. This is seeing who we are, without the shadow of 'I' and 'my.' This brightness trades the crutch of 'why' for the true ground of 'why not,' the absolute firmness of 'because.' It is the wonderful security not of having something under our feet but of having something over our heads. Hence the idea that what is firm—the firmament—is not our foundation but rather our roof and the idea of 'up above.'

Our real way out is not the light at the end of the tunnel, as our natural expectations tell us. It can be found anywhere in the tunnel. It is a paradoxical guarantee gained not from a feeling of control and permanence but of transience. It is the security acquired by whoever guides his life by the notion of 'if not now, when?' Whoever conducts himself in this fashion discovers that each moment is an end in itself. And then it matters little where you're going. All you have to do is make the same into something different, and if you are anywhere, you can leave anywhere.

A way out is the choice which fear-transformed-into-action steadily offers us. And this transformation becomes possible through intelligence which makes us see that when our passage on the outside are blocked the way out is to be found inside. This inside knows paths out, and this outside knows paths in, and thanks to these options, walls and obstacles are torn down. This outside doesn't take us any place—much less home—but it fosters encounters. So it is the outside which teaches us that the role of light is not to help us find a way out but to promote encounters. Because we believe light shows us things when in reality it reflects. Everything we see is the reflection of something placed in light. They are experiences of encounters much more than exposure to true essences. So light does not reveal—rather, it acts as the intermediary between the inside and the outside.

True clarity does not come from seeing yourself, but in knowing before you know and not letting this very light fool you. What blinds us is not darkness but whatever obscures. And our desire for light distorts and misleads. Our egos, for example, are a product of this distortion. They derive their origin from our eyes, whose vision is obscured by the impression we're better than we imagine. And thus we need our eyelids, the private blindness of knowing we are also worse than we imagine—and this gives us rest and relief.

By constantly obscuring things, light engenders such vision problems as fear, mistrust, and confusion. Nothing could then be better than a tear to moisten and blur our vision, lending greater 'visibility' to the understanding that we see more through truth and experience than through certainty. Certainty does violence against us, making us albinos in a luminous world of power and answers.

What we see is a comment on reality and not reality itself. This is why darkness can bring us closer to the source and origin, without interference from mirages or distortions. In darkness, we find that contradictions like these make sense: the more we are alone, the more we are together; equality lies in difference; 'plus' does not always add up. In darkness we understand that the opposite is not the contrary. That life, for example, does not stand in opposition to death but to immortality. That pleasure does not stand in opposition to pain but to comfort. After all, the one who needs to distinguish in order to see is vision, and everything that 'is' must contrast with an 'isn't.' This means that good luminance draws in shadows, because darkness is part of the image as a pause is part of time.

Lucky is the rooster, who sings the day in the midst of night. For him there are no contradictions, since light fades into twilight, and terrifying into dawn. His role is to sing early every morning, trying to awaken the world, but not to bring the day, as we usually think. He sings instead to awaken us to the fact that night breaks into day. He alerts us to a portal that opens daily in teaching. It is the moment when those lost in the forest find light. And they think this light puts an end to their exile. But day can be just as deceptive as the dark, perhaps more so. Light is no good for seeing, much less for showing ways out. It draws us closer to the blind man so he can soothe us. The rooster sings to show us that the forest, night, and fear are not in themselves real. And that the nightmare which was real until just a very little while ago finds us at home, in our bed, tucked beneath our blankets.

Bibliography

Anthology of Jewish Mysticism, Raphael Ben Zion (ed.), Judaica Press
Back to the Sources, Barry W. Holz, Jewish Publication Society
The Book of Legends, H. N. Bialikm, Schocken Books
Classic Hassidic Stories, Meyer Lewin, Penguin Books
Cutting Through Spiritual Materialism, Chogyam Trungpa, Shambhala
The Enlightened Heart, Stephen Mitchell, HarperPerennial
For the Sake of Heaven, Martin Buber, Atheneum
God Desired and Desiring, Juan Ramon Jimenez, Paragon House
The Herschel Tradition, Moshe Braun, Jason Aronson
Learning from the Tanya, Adin Steinsaltz, Jossey-Bass
Luminous Emptiness, Francesca Fremantle, Shambhala
The Maggid Speaks, J. Krohne, Mesorah Publication
Meeting with Remarkable Souls, Eliahu Klein, Jason Aronson
New Seeds of Contemplation, Thomas Merton, New Directions Books
Present At Sinai, S. Y. Agnon, Jewish Publication Society
Rabbi Nachman's Stories, Aryeh Kaplan, Breslov
Roads to the Palace, Michael Rosenak, Berghahn Books
The Sayings of Kotsk, Raz Levin, Aronson
The Search of the Beloved, Jean Houston, St. Martin's Press
Spiritual Intimacy, Zalman Schachter Shalomi, Jason Aronson
Whestling With Angels, Naomi Rosenblatt, Delacorte Press